Rev. Andreas Michai........
(of the Church of Thyateira and Gr. Britain)
of the Ecumenical Patriarchate

THE CREED

THE NEW AND PERFECT REVELATION OF GOD IN JESUS CHRIST

(A MODERN ANALYSIS)

Second edition

Nottingham 2011

xulon
PRESS

*To George
my brother in Christ*

THE CREED

THE NEW AND PERFECT REVELATION OF GOD IN JESUS CHRIST

(A MODERN ANALYSIS)

Second edition

*With the love of Jesus Christ
Father Andreas*

Copyright © 2011 by Rev. Andreas Michailidis

The Creed
The New and Perfect Revelation of God in Jesus Christ
by Rev. Andreas Michailidis

Printed in the United States of America

ISBN 9781613791585

All rights reserved solely by the author. The author guarantees all contents are original and do not infringe upon the legal rights of any other person or work. No part of this book may be reproduced in any form without the permission of the author. The views expressed in this book are not necessarily those of the publisher.

Unless otherwise indicated, Bible quotations are taken from The New King James Version of THE ORTHODOX STUDY BIBLE, New Testament and Psalms. Copyright © 1993 by Thomas Nelson Publishers, Nashville, Tennessee.

© Rev Andreas Michailidis
24 Hawksley Gardens
Barton Green
Nottingham
NG11 8SU
UK
Tel. (0044)1159406013
Fax (0044) 115 9406245
Email: andreas.michailidis@tinyworld.co.uk

Copy Editor: Rev. Andreas Michailidis
Editor and catalogue designer: E. Kanakis
Composition: Miliou Konstantina
Production: Grapholine (Tel. (0030) 231 0 250584)

www.xulonpress.com

†

This book is dedicated to the memory
of my son Anastasios
who belongs to the triumphant
heavenly Church.
It is also dedicated to all those who are striving
to find the real Truth and the true Life in order to
become citizens of the Kingdom of God.

Father Andreas

CONTENTS

†

Prologue xiii
Introduction xvii
The Creed (in Greek) xxi
The Creed (in English) xxiii
Article 1 25
Article 2 43
Article 3 59
Article 4 96
Article 5 115
Article 6 125
Article 7 130
Article 8 151
Article 9 175
Article 10 192
Article 11 198
Article 12 204
Epilogue 211

†

NOTE: The reader will find that certain items are repeated. This is done for two reasons:

a. To consolidate these important truths in the mind of the reader and
b. So that the reader who chooses to read any article in the book separately, will not miss these basic truths.

PROLOGUE

✝

This work began when the writer commenced his Bible sessions with his parishioners in Nottingham, England, in 2001. He began with a rather comprehensive introduction to the study of the Bible before entering the main work of analyzing the books of the New Testament and the Psalms.

When he reached the point of dealing with the Creed, he realized how immense the subject was and started dealing with its analysis. Finally, he reached the point of writing a whole work: the book you are holding in your hands.

The writer thought that it was his duty, as a theologian and as a priest, to let his parishioners, and as many Christians as possible, know more about what they usually say when they recite the Creed. Sometimes they recite it without really knowing what they are really saying; or if they do they know very little. Sometimes what they think they know is wholly or partially wrong.

The writer knows that he is not the first to write about the Creed. He merely thought of giving his own interpretation of the Creed, especially based on his theological research dealing with the concept of space and time, within the framework of the solution of the theological problem about the existence or not of a middle state of the souls. That is why the writer thinks that this is a modern interpretation of the Creed. This does not mean innovations that go beyond the 'limits' of our faith; that would be absolutely contradictory to the essence of the present undertaking, which deals with the Creed. The Creed means the revealed truths that we believe in and these truths cannot change or be modified in any way through the ages.

Whatever the writer says here is not his knowledge but it is based hopefully on the wisdom of the Fathers of our Church whom he has studied diligently.

The writer also asks to be forgiven for any flaws in his writing. One might find errors in the language. English is not his mother tongue. Of course, one may spot some other more serious errors. In such a case, the writer would consider great help not only for him but his readers, that you may contact him and tell him about them. A potential third edition would prove better than this one. A mention of those who will contribute towards a better third edition will be made.

It was not at all an easy venture to deal with the Creed. However, the writer had such an overwhelming inner urge to write this work that it was irresistible.

It was not easy, because the Creed is the heart of our faith and it contains its most profound elements. An analysis of these elements is one of the most difficult tasks that one could attempt to make. At the same time, it is one the most useful and vital ones. Our people sometimes do not know their faith. They sometimes recite the Creed without knowing what they are saying. They consider all these things that they read some kind of inaccessible mystery of our 'religion' that is there for us just to read but not to know what it is all about. By the way, sometimes religion is combined with an attitude of this kind. And our faith, when it is rendered into a religion, resembles something like that.

However, we all know very well that the Creed is not supposed to be something like that. The Creed is the basis of our faith. If we do not know what it says, then we are not real Christians. It is as simple as that. And the more we know about it, the more genuine Christians we are, if we could evaluate our faith.

And there is something else; this book was also written for all those non-Christian people who would like to know what our faith is. They have the right to know. It is unforgivable for us Christians that we have not made our faith known to everybody. It is our duty to do that even now. Unfortunately, today a lot of Christians would consider something like that as a kind of proselytism. The latter is not the case here. We do not in any way force anybody to accept our faith. If making our faith known to as many people as possible were a kind of proselytism, then the apostles would be considered as having done something contemptible. However, we know very well that they did not. The world actually owes them a great deal for their work of spreading the good tidings of our salvation.

The least we can do for our world today is to make our faith known to all peoples of the world with all kinds of means that we have available: radio, television, books, the internet, videos and in so many other ways. God has provided us with so many means of spreading His gospel to the world that we have no excuse of not doing it. The only excuse is that we perhaps do not really and profoundly believe in what we say that we do. This is the most probable case. The people of the world are most ready today to listen to the Gospel but they want to hear it from the mouths of believing people who really live out their faith. Otherwise our words would be a 'wooden language'. People are tired of our 'wooden language', the language that sounds so terrible in the ears of people. It is a great blasphemy to utter the name of Jesus Christ, our God, in such a language. The name of Jesus Christ, our God, is the name that is above all names; it is the most holy name and it must be pronounced by the lips of persons who are overwhelmed by feelings of devotion towards Him. One must be shaken with one's faith in all of the articles of the Creed that we shall attempt to analyze here.

INTRODUCTION

†

The Creed is the basis of our faith. It is the product of the first two ecumenical synods. The third ecumenical synod consolidated the Creed. Its resolution was that no word could be deducted or added to the Creed as it was formulated during the first two ecumenical synods. We shall see below how important that was and is for safeguarding the genuineness of our faith.

The fact that the Creed was formulated during the first two ecumenical synods is of vital importance. As the Apostolic Synod bears more importance than the ecumenical synods, so the first ecumenical synods are more important than the later ones. This is so because the closer to the times of Jesus and the Apostles we are the closer to the truth we are found.

For the formulation of the Creed, a great role should be attributed to the heresies. No matter how strange this might sound, without heresies we would not have the Creed and all the dogmas of our Church. Heresies 'forced' the Church to go along and do what they did. The true faith was there and it is all the time. However, it has to be provoked in order for it to be formulated into dogmas. The latter are nothing else but the truths of our faith clearly stated.

The first ecumenical synod formulated the first seven articles of our faith. The second one formulated the articles eight to twelve.

What made our Church convene and decide and formulate the first seven articles of the Creed was basically the heresy of Arius. Arius asserted that Jesus was not God; for him Jesus was a created being like us who was sent by God to us to reveal certain truths. Therefore, the object of Arius's attack was Jesus Christ. Arianism, Arius's heresy, contributed greatly to the formulation of Christology, that is: the branch of Theology (or dogmatics) which deals with the person of Christ. That is why the first seven articles (or even more precisely from article two to article seven) deal with the person of Jesus. It is important for us to know absolutely well who Christ is. Otherwise our faith would be void of any substance. At least, we would waver in our faith. We would not have a steadfast faith. An unstable faith is a contradictory thing. How could one believe in something but not be absolutely sure about it?

Therefore, we owe a lot to the first ecumenical synod for providing us with this necessary teaching for the steadfastness of our faith articles about the person of Jesus Christ. For us Christians, the person of Jesus is of vital importance. He is the saviour of Man. Without Him there would not be any Kingdom of God for us; there would not be any salvation. If Jesus were not God, the Son of God, consubstantial with the Father, then not only could He not save us but He would need a saviour Himself.

The first article tells us what we believe concerning the first person of the Holy Trinity. Our Creed could not ignore Him. Although the first ecumenical synod dealt with the second person of the Holy Trinity, it would have to deal with the first person first. How could they logically deal with the second person without any reference whatsoever to the first person? The reference to the first person serves another purpose as well. The second person is the Son of God. Who is this person, though, that Jesus is the Son of? To be a son you must have a father. Sonship without fathership cannot exist. It was necessary then to start from the Father. The Father also makes the oneness of God more concrete. Yes, I believe in one God. This God is the Father. The Father of whom? The answer to this question comes very naturally with the second article which tells us what we believe about the second person of the Holy Trinity, that is: the Son of the Father.

The second ecumenical synod dealt with the Third Person of the Holy Trinity. Again here a heresy 'forced' the Church to formulate the eighth article, which deals with our faith about the Holy Spirit. The cause for the formulation of this article was the heresy of those who fought against the divinity of the Holy Spirit. Those heretics asserted that the Holy Spirit is not God in nature and does not have the same substance with the Father and the Son. That is why the second ecumenical synod was convened and formulated the eighth article of the Creed which deals solely with the Third Person of the Holy Trinity: the Holy Spirit.

Having been convened, the second ecumenical synod decided on other articles of our faith as well: a) what we believe about the essence of the Church, b) what we believe about baptism, c) what we believe about the Resurrection and d) about eternal life.

Before we begin dealing with the Creed, let us pray together with St. Dionysius the Areopagite, as he does in his treatise *On Mystical Theology*:

'Trinity, super-substantial and over-divine and over-benevolent; you that guard from up there on high the knowledge of the Christians about the divine things, lead us into the mystical 'words' of the more than unknown and more than brilliant and most extreme apex; there where the supreme darkness of mystical quiet covers the simple and the absolute and never-changing theological mysteries; there where its darkness shines more than light and, in an entirely unknown and invisible manner, fills the angelic powers with more than brilliant grandeur' (Dionysius Areopagite, *On Mystical Theology - Introduction by Vladimir Lossky (in Greek) ed. by Philosophos Logos, Polytypo 1983, Athens).*

ΤΟ ΣΥΜΒΟΛΟ ΤΗΣ ΠΙΣΤΕΩΣ

†

Άρθρο 1ο   Πιστεύω εις ένα Θεόν, Πατέρα, παντοκράτορα, ποιητήν ουρανού και γης, ορατών τε πάντων και αοράτων.

Άρθρο 2ο   Και εις ένα Κύριον Ιησούν Χριστόν, τον Υιόν του Θεού τον μονογενή, τον εκ του Πατρός γεννηθέντα προ πάντων των αιώνων. Φως εκ Φωτός, Θεόν αληθινόν εκ Θεού Αληθινού γεννηθέντα, ου ποιηθέντα, ομοούσιον τω Πατρί, δι ού τα πάντα εγένετο.

Άρθρο 3ο   Τον δι' ημάς τους ανθρώπους και διά την ημετέραν σωτηρίαν κατελθόντα εκ των ουρανών και σαρκωθέντα εκ Πνεύματος Αγίου και Μαρίας της Παρθένου και ενανθρωπήσαντα.

Άρθρο 4ο   Σταυρωθέντα τε υπέρ ημών επί Ποντίου Πιλάτου και παθόντα και ταφέντα

Άρθρο 5ο	Και αναστάντα τη τρίτη ημέρα, κατά τας Γραφάς.
Άρθρο 6ο	Και ανελθόντα εις τους ουρανούς και καθεζόμενον εκ δεξιών του Πατρός.
Άρθρο 7ο	Και πάλιν ερχόμενον μετά δόξης κρίναι ζώντας και νεκρούς, ού της Βασιλείας ουκ έσται τέλος.
Άρθρο 8ο	Και εις το Πνεύμα το Άγιον, το Κύριον, το ζωοποιόν, το εκ του Πατρός εκπορευόμενον, το συν Πατρί και Υιώ συμπροσκυνούμενον και συνδοξαζόμενον, το λαλήσαν διά των προφητών.
Άρθρο 9ο	Εις μίαν, αγίαν, καθολικήν και αποστολικήν Εκκλησίαν.
Άρθρο 10ο	Ομολογώ έν βάπτισμα εις άφεσιν αμαρτιών.
Άρθρο 11ο	Προσδοκώ ανάστασιν νεκρών.
Άρθρο 12ο	Και ζωήν του μέλλοντος αιώνος. Αμήν.

THE CREED

✝

Article 1   I believe in one God, Father almighty, maker of heaven and earth, and of all things visible and invisible.

Article 2   And in one Lord Jesus Christ, the only begotten Son of God, begotten from the Father before all ages. Light from Light, true God from true God, begotten not made, consubstantial with the Father, through Him all things were made.

Article 3   For our sake and for our salvation he came down from Heaven, and was incarnate from the Holy Spirit and the Virgin Mary and became man.

Article 4   He was crucified also for us under Pontius Pilate, and suffered and was buried.

Article 5   He rose again on the third day, in accordance with the Scriptures.

Article 6	And ascended into Heaven, and is seated at the right hand of the Father.
Article 7	He is coming again in glory to judge the living and the dead and His Kingdom will have no end.
Article 8	And in the Holy Spirit, the Lord, the Giver of Life, who proceeds from the Father, who together with Father and Son is worshipped and together glorified; who spoke through the prophets.
Article 9	In One, Holy, Catholic and Apostolic Church.
Article 10	I confess one baptism for the forgiveness of sins.
Article 11	I await the resurrection of the dead.
Article 12	And the life of the age to come. Amen.

Article 1

I believe in one God, Father Almighty, Maker of heaven and earth, and of all things visible and invisible;

✝

I believe in one God,

I believe

I! Who is *I*? A mystery. It is true that each one of us is a whole mystery; a mystery that is extremely difficult to explore. Yet, it is worth investigating. Even the ancient Greeks were able to establish that this mystery needs and is really worth our attention. ΄*Γνῶθι σαυτόν*΄ "Know thyself", they used to say. Socrates was able to do that to a great extent. And as he is telling us, he was able to hear God's voice deep in there, that is: in the most profound depths of his inner world. Actually, Socrates was able, better than anyone else, to know Man through this search of his.

I is a whole world; an unexplored world. *I*'s origin; *I*'s development; *I*'s co-existence with the individual or rather personal *self*. The existence of a whole inner world, with a most subtle function; with its conscience, both psychological and moral; with its potencies and potentialities and a vast number of other factors: passions and the like, render *I* into a most intricate world. Yet, the *I* is each one of us. Nobody would be able to know *I* better than the one who is identical with it. Every and each one of us knows, to a certain extent, his or her personal *I*. And not only knows it, but is striving to know it better. This is the best case, yet a very rare one. The common case is the effort that each one makes **not to know** his or her *I*. The reasons are many: most do not like dealing with complicated matters like this. Or they do not like what they see there, deep in it. Others find it a very obscure matter.

Finally, it is this *I* that we are striving to help to get into the Kingdom of Heaven. And it is this *I* that believes or disbelieves.

I **believe**. Belief is a universal matter. It embraces all fields of life. We would not be able to do anything if we did not have some kind of belief or trust in what we decide to do. Without it, we would not be able to do even the most banal or commonplace things. We would not even step out of our homes if we did not believe that that would be a safe thing to do. We would never step into any shop to buy anything if we did not believe that the people in there would serve us appropriately, sell us the right thing and charge us fairly. We would not put our money in a bank, if we did not think that it would be safe there and that we would be able to draw it at any time that we wished with interest, too.

In the case that we are going to deal with, the belief is a religious function. What comes after it, is '**in one God**'. Therefore, there is no doubt that we are dealing with religious belief or rather faith.

As we mentioned above, belief or faith is a kind of trust. A belief in someone or something is the simple trust in him/her or it. I trust him and that is why I am lending him some money. I am trusting her, I trust her love towards me, and that is why I marry her. I trust the good construction and maintenance of the roads, the traffic laws and the whole traffic system and that is why I am found driving along the road going somewhere. Therefore, when I say "I believe in God", I mean that I trust Him.

However, whereas I know what I mean by trusting this or that person and so on, I do not always know what I mean by saying "I trust God". What is really this kind of trust?

Let us give an example. When a mother is holding a baby in her arms singing lullabies for it to get to sleep, sometimes she feels that its weight has increased a little. Just then, she takes a look at it and finds out that her baby has just gone to sleep. Its very slight increase in weight is due to the fact that it has wholly surrendered in her arms. We might say that the baby naturally has a complete trust in its mother. There is nothing to fear from her, just because she is its mother. It loves her more than anything or anyone else in this world. Actually, she is the world for it.

In the same but a superior way, man believes in God. Man trusts God more than anybody else; and loves Him more than anybody or anything else. The believing Man surrenders entirely in the 'arms' of God. And that is so, because Man has nothing to fear from Him or even from anybody or anything else. Man does not fear God. We have heard of fear of God and how Man must have this kind of fear. However, this should go along with an explanation. This kind of fear has no relation whatsoever with the fear that we know of. It would even be a blasphemy thinking of such kind of fear being applied to God. We are not afraid of God the way people are afraid of fearsome persons or things. When we say fear in relation to God, we mean this kind of reverence and mystical awe that we have in us when we are communicating with or contemplating about God. We know our position in life and our natural and essential and vast difference from Him. We are created beings; He is uncreated. We have a beginning and a natural end; He has no beginning and no end. We have life that is given to us from Him; He is the Life Himself. We exist because He wanted us to come into existence. He is Existence Itself.

We shall see why we are not afraid of Him in a little. We do not fear Him, because we love Him. And as St. John says 'Perfect love casts fear out' (I John 4.18).

In conclusion, when I say 'I believe', I mean that I trust God entirely and I love Him more than anybody or anything else. Actually, my trust in Him and my love for Him are incomparable to any other kind of trust or love.

in one God,

In. When I believe, I believe **in** someone or something. I do not just believe. The belief or trust should necessarily have an object. You trust someone or something; you do not just trust.

It is different when we are talking about someone who, for example, believes or shows trust easily. When that credulous person finally (even easily) believes, he believes **in** someone or something. And by the way, when I believe in God, that is not a matter of credulity. It is an achievement of the **I**. It is the **I** who, through doubts, searches and researches, studying and contemplating, has reached this state of belief or faith. Because belief or faith is really a kind of condition or state. It is, one might say, a whole world in which the faithful lives. His experiences in this world are unique and entirely unknown by the non-believer. The true believer is actually not at all the credulous type. He is exactly the opposite. He resembles rather the doubting Thomas. He wants to put his finger into the print of the nails and thrust his hand into Jesus' side in order to believe. The believer that is the credulous type usually (but not always) has a very superficial faith. But a doubting Thomas who has at last managed to find the truth for himself is more liable to be a very strong and dedicated believer.

One. God cannot be of any other number but one. Why? Even philosophers were able to establish that fact through the logic of philosophy. If we suppose that there are several gods, then they should owe their existence to some other gods or god. Finally, we reach the point where there is only one God, because then we cannot ask the question 'who does He owe His existence to?' simply because there is no one else behind Him. He is the only one. And, of course, again, He is everlasting, that is: there was no time that He did not exist, because then one might ask: 'and how did He acquire existence?' And, of course, because of that, He has no end.

However, we must discriminate the oneness of God we believe in from the oneness of God of some religions, like Allah of Islam. The latter is one god but not the same as ours. As we shall see later on, our God is Trinity. He is One but three Persons.

Philosophy of Religion considers Christianity as one of the monotheistic religions. Monotheism is the belief in one God. We do not absolutely agree with the aspect of Philosophy of Religion. Unfortunately, all sciences which deal with the phenomenon of religion treat Christianity as one of the religions of the world. We do not agree with them in the idea that our faith is a religion. Therefore, we do not absolutely accept the term Christianity when it sounds like a religion. We do not consider religion as something to pour scorn on. On the contrary, religion is the praiseworthy endeavour of Man to elevate himself as high as possible in order to reach Man's creator and God. However, Man's endeavour is doomed to fail, because it was Man that separated himself from God and lost touch with Him. Therefore, only God could help Man, through revelation, to really reach God.

This revelation can be found only in the Bible; through the Old Testament partially at first and then fully in the New Testament, through and in Jesus Christ, the Son of God. The Son of God takes human nature in the one and only person of Jesus Christ. Therefore, there is no need for Man to do what religions do. According to our faith as Christians, God is not far from Man. God is among His people and He is united with them. In religion Man reaches as high as possible, in a desperate fashion, without finally finding true God. In our faith, the opposite happens: true God comes down to earth to reveal Himself and to be reunited with Man. In other words, our faith is the end of religion. There is no need for religion. How could we then call religion that which is the end of religion?

Unfortunately, our faith sometimes has come to be a religion with the wear of time and the tendency of Man to turn his faith into religion. It is much easier for Man to use religious ways to 'communicate' with Man's creator. However, this is inexcusable, because it is unreasonable to consider or turn into religion what is supposed to be the end of religion. It is a blasphemy to consider Jesus Christ as one of the founders of religions and Christianity being one of them. Jesus is not a founder of a religion. He is the incarnate Son of God, the saviour of the world.

What is our faith, then? In the New Testament, not even once do we encounter the word Christianity or that our faith is a religion. On the contrary, we can see very clearly that our faith is the New Creation, the New Israel, which is in Heaven. The first Christians

The Creed

---

were persecuted because (among other reasons) they were 'atheists', according to the standards of those times. The reason was because the faith of the Christians was not a religion. In those times of syncretism, religions were not only not persecuted but they were very much appreciated.

The first Christian Church was separated from Judaism. One of the reasons was that Judaism was and is a religion.

What is our faith, then? When St. Paul wanted to give it a name, he called it The Way. He says: 'But this I confess to you, that according to the **Way,** which they call a sect, so I worship the God of my fathers...'(Acts 24.14), and then 'But when Felix heard these things, having more accurate knowledge of the **Way**...' (Acts 24.22) and also 'I persecuted this **Way** to the death, binding and delivering into prisons both men and women" (22.4). Therefore, our faith is not a religion; it is the **Way**. It is the only way that can lead Man not only to communion with God but into union with God as well. We can also call it **Ecclesia** (the Church). When we say Ecclesia, we mean the gathering of all those who believe and are united with Him round the same table of the Mystical Last Supper. There, we sit next to the apostles, being apostles of His as well, and we accept His sacrifice before our eyes and we understand even more than His first apostles. We accept from His own hands His Body and His Blood. We take them down into our body and soul and in this way we are united with Him, the Son of God, God Himself. We are the **New Creation**. Within our faith, we are found on the right **Way** leading to Heavens, the Kingdom of God; we are **Ecclesia**, the body of Christ. Therefore, we are members of the Body of Christ. The world we live in, as Christians, is no longer what it used to be or what is for anyone who is not a member of His Body. The world we live in, as Christians, is the world that was created on the night of Jesus' birth. Heavens were drawn down to earth and have become one unity. Space and time take a completely other form. As far as space is concerned, the church, as a building, tells us what the Church is. Its floor represents the earth on which we still are; the dome represents heaven which is our destiny and which has been drawn down to earth; the iconostasis is the ladder through which we climb up to Heaven. As far as time is concerned, we have a transformation of it. For the Church, time, which is a temporal and therefore a temporary measure, does not have its usual dimensions: past/present/future. Within the Church, time is a perpetual present. In this way we have a 'taste' of eternity. Our faith is thus also a **<u>Unity of Heaven and earth</u>**. That is why we have icons or representations of all Heavenly Church (Jesus, Virgin Mary, St. John the Baptist, of all the saints, of the angels) inside our church buildings. We do not merely have the sense or the feeling that all the Heavenly Church is there with us (the earthly Church), but we are certain about it. We experience this very reality every time that we are found in church gathered all together with the company of the heavenly powers and particularly of Jesus, His Mother and of all the saints and all the departed members of the Church who are in Heaven.

The Creed

In conclusion, we believe in one God, not in the way that Philosophy of Religion teaches concerning monotheism. We believe in one God in the way our Church experiences in the three Persons of the Holy Trinity, with whom we are going to deal below.

And this brings us to **God**. The Creed starts with: 'I believe in one God'. 'And who is this God that you believe in?' one might ask. The answer to this question is extremely difficult. This is due to the fact that there is no definition of God. We might define almost anything that exists either in the world or even in our mind; we might even give the definitions of things or persons that do not exist but which exist in our imagination or as ideas. Yet, we are incapable of defining God. That is one of the reasons why people were predominantly idolatrous before Christ. The sole exemption were the Jews. They believed in the one true God. How was this so?

We all know now that Man was created by the unique and only one God. We all know that Man was separated from God with his fall. From then onwards Man gradually becomes completely ignorant of God. That was why they were idolaters. They knew deep inside them that they must owe their existence to some superior power or powers. They did not know exactly who. Therefore, they guessed and they worshipped either imaginary gods or animals or things that they supposed that they had some kind of supernatural power in them. There was only the exemption that was mentioned above: the Jews.

How did they know the true God? This is the great difference in comparison to all the other peoples: God revealed Himself to the Jews. Now, there remains one more question to be answered: 'Why did God reveal Himself to them?' The reason was that God did not want to lose all contact with the race of Man. He had His plans for the salvation of Man. Now, there remains one more and final question: 'Why the Jews? What made Him choose them among all the other peoples of the world?' The answer to this question is strange and a little difficult for someone to accept. The reason was one person: his name: Abraham.

Why was he the reason that God chose the nation of the Jews to carry out His plan for the salvation of Man? As there is one person through whom God 'manages' to carry out His dispensation, that is: the Virgin Mary, so Abraham was the reason why God chose the nation of Israel to be the chosen nation. Abraham was a person devoted to God. He was so devoted that he even obeyed Him and decided to sacrifice his son. Above, we dealt with faith. Well, Abraham is the unique person in the History of Man before Christ that had so much faith in God. He was the Man of Faith.

Father almighty

Why **'Father'**? We all know what 'father' means. Is God a father? Of course, one might argue, that the Creed does not say just a common father, because the first letter is written with a capital F. 'Therefore,' one might say, 'yes, God is a father but not a regular father, but an extraordinary kind of father. He is the father of everybody.'

However, the first thing that we might say is that the use of this word is not exhaustive of what we mean. There is no word that might suffice in describing God. This is very often said. An instance of this is what the priest reads in the mystical prayer of *Anaphora or Holy Oblation*: 'for you are God ineffable, incomprehensible, invisible, inconceivable, ever existing, eternally the same;' He is *ineffable*. We cannot actually utter one word that could be appropriate or which would rightly express what God is. So, even the word *Father,* no matter how capital the F is, could not express what God is. Therefore, we must always have in mind that whatever we say in relation to God, even the word God itself cannot express what really He is.

One might ask, why then do we use these words? The answer is that we have no choice. Or rather, the only other choice that we have is not to say anything about Him; not even utter His name. But then we cannot do that. We cannot shut our mouth and say nothing about Him to whom we owe everything, even our existence. So, we resolve the problem by using human words just because we do not know any other language. If we knew the language of the angels we might use it. Even then, there is a doubt whether that would be absolutely sufficient.

Another thing that we might say about the word *Father* is that it is a word that expresses, to some extent, what He is to us. As we owe

The Creed

our birth to our earthly father, all of us do owe our true existence to Him. Without His will, we would not exist. Nobody and nothing would exist.

The fact that He is our Father is proven by Our Lord's prayer as well. There we say, 'Our Father who are in Heaven'. So, we know that He is our Father, not the one that is on earth, but the One Who is in Heaven. The fact that this prayer was given to the Apostles by our Lord Himself and was then handed from generation to generation to us, shows the truth of the fact; the fact that He is our Father.

We have this relation between us and God in the Old Testament as well. Such examples are: 'God, Father and Lord of my life' (Sirach: 23.1), 'Because He is our Lord and God, He is our Father in all ages' (Tob. 13.4), 'Father God' (Wsd 2.16) and in innumerable other places. In the New Testament, we have even more cases like these. Jesus Himself gives the prayer in which we address God as our Father. In Matthew's chapter 6, we have several cases where God is called our Father, starting from the line 48 of the previous chapter 5, where Jesus says: 'Therefore you shall be perfect, just as your Father in Heaven is perfect'.

However there is another signification of the Father. And this is even more important. The Father is the first person of the Holy Trinity. He is also, and mainly so, the Father of our Lord Jesus Christ. However, He is not like the Father that He is in relation to us.

First of all, that He is Jesus' Father, we know from the words of Jesus Himself. In Matthew 11.27, Jesus says: 'All things have been delivered to Me by My Father; and no one knows the Son except the Father. Nor does anyone know the Father except the Son, and the one to whom the Son wills to reveal Him'. Yet the highest revelation of the fact that Jesus is the Son of God, the second person of the Holy Trinity can be found in John 17.21: 'that they all may be one, as You, Father, are in Me, and I in You'. And a little below, 17.24: 'Father, I desire that they also, whom You gave Me may be with Me where I am, that they may behold My glory, which You have given Me; for You loved Me before the foundation of the world'.

All the above and many other evidences of the special Sonship of Jesus in relation to the Father will be useful for the analysis of the Creed concerning Jesus Christ, our Lord.

Another very important factor should be mentioned here as well: the fact that the Father is the first person of the Holy Trinity. Certainly, the idea of His being the first does not mean that He is more important and greater than the other two persons; and therefore, that there is inequity among the three persons. The Father does not beget His Son in order that the latter be of less importance than Himself. And He does not send forth the Holy Spirit in such a way that It be of an inferior standard than Him. The Son is begotten and the Holy Spirit is sent forth so that they may be of equal standing as the Father. Of course, there should not be any confusion among the three. They are distinguished as we men are distinguished between one another and there is no case of somebody confusing one with the other even in the case of identical twins.

Concerning the equality that exists among the three persons we might mention also the fact that God wants even men, who are created beings, ultimately to partake of His greatness and be equal to Him. This is concluded from the fact that Jesus says: 'that they (the apostles) all may be one, as You Father, are in Me, and I in You; that they also may be one in Us' (John 17.21).

However, we must never forget that the Father is the first person. That means a lot. It means that He is the source of divinity and that He has pre-eminent roles within the divinity. An example of that is that everything depends on His will. Without it there would not be any Son being begotten and no Holy Spirit being sent forth. The creation of the worlds, the spiritual and the material, are due to the fact that He wanted them to be created. Of course, the will of God does not come under the same category as our will. First of all, the will of God does not fall within the framework of time and space, as happens with our will. When we want something, this happens somewhere and at some particular time. This is not the case with the will of God. His will is timeless.

The fact that everything depends on the Father's will is proven in several instances. One of them is the case of the creation of the worlds that was mentioned above. Another proof is the fact of the work of our salvation. If the Father did not want us to be saved, He would not have sent His Son to the world to save us. In John 17.18 we read: 'as You sent Me into the world,' as well in John 3.16: 'For

God so loved the world that He gave His only begotten Son, that whoever believes in Him should not perish but have everlasting life'.

Another fundamental attribute of the Father is that He is Love, the absolute and inconceivable Love. He shows that in many ways. What brings forth His Son is actually this Love. And that is the reason why His Son is also Love itself since He is the product of His Father's Love. And the Holy Spirit is the Father's Love also that comes out of Him in the greatest abundance. Actually, all divinity shines in this Third Person, that is: the Holy Spirit. Without it, nothing would function right and nothing would have life in it. However, we should never forget that the two other persons of divinity are due to the Father.

Now, we come to **almighty**. One of the attributes of God is that He is almighty or omnipotent. There is nothing that God wants and cannot do. He is the only One that can create things, that is: He can make things from nothing. This is the greatest power that He has. There is actually nothing that He would not be able to do. The only thing that He cannot do is to go against His own will. And that of course is very natural.

God has several attributes; all good ones. It is these attributes of God that render us able to know God. We cannot know God in His essence; we may know Him only through His energies. And these energies are responsible for our giving Him these attributes. For instance, we see His creation and we gather that He is almighty, most wise, most benevolent and many other attributes.

The Creed

In this case, we mention this attribute of His, because of what is going to follow:

Maker of Heaven and earth

He is the **maker**. What do we mean by that? Is He a maker like the makers of things that we know of? Of course not. God does not 'work' in the way we do. For instance, He does not need any tools to make something. All He 'needs' is His Word or Logos. And that is where the second person of the Holy Trinity, the Father's Son, comes in. The Father does not proceed in doing anything in His person. He does everything through His Son, who is His Word. His Word (or Logos) is not like our word. It is not an utterance. It is the second person of the Holy Trinity. And again His Word does not make things in the way we do. The Word (the Logos) does not have any hands or tools to make things. As He is almighty, by just His existence, things are made. And not just plain things but whole worlds: the spiritual and the material ones. The spiritual world is what we express with the word *Heaven*; the material one is what we express with the word *earth* and in general the universe. The fact that the word *Heaven* denotes the spiritual world is evident from what follows in the Creed:

and of all things visible and invisible

The order of the words *visible* and *invisible* is not like the one that we have above. The word *visible* refers to the word *earth* and the word *invisible* refers to the word *Heaven*.

Let us start from the second word: *invisible*. As we mentioned above, this refers to Heaven. This is the spiritual world. This world belongs to eternity and it is the second light. According to St. Gregory, the Theologian, the first Light is God Himself. The second light are the angels. And the third light is Man.

This is so because the angels are a purely spiritual creation and therefore are closer to the nature of God. Whereas Man is a combination of both the spiritual and the material world.

The spiritual world is characterized as invisible. Why? Because it cannot be perceived with our eyes. We know that in order to see something, certain factors must be there. One of them is the stimulus. The other factor is the eye. The eye is the receptor of the stimulus. And, of course, there must be the brain to which the reception of the stimulus will be sent. And the brain must, of course, contain the right centre to receive the stimulus and that centre must be ready and suitable to process the stimulus in order to produce the image that is 'translated' into what we say that we see.

Article 2

And in one Lord, Jesus Christ, the only begotten Son of God, begotten from the Father before all ages, Light from Light, true God from true God, begotten not made, consubstantial with the Father, through Him all things were made.

✝

And in one Lord, Jesus Christ,

And

What we have just gone through was the first article of our faith. Now we are going to deal with the second article. There are actually twelve articles in all.

The first article concerns the first person of the Holy Trinity. The second, third, fourth, fifth, sixth and seventh articles concern the second person of the Holy Trinity, that is: our Lord Jesus Christ, the only-begotten Son of God.

The word **and** that it begins with actually means: in addition to the fact that I believe in the Father, I also believe in the second person of the Holy Trinity. And who is this?

in one Lord,

The second person of the Holy Trinity is *unique* as the Father is. And He is wholly distinguished from the first person. And not only that; He is the **Lord**. What about the Father? Isn't He the Lord as well? Of course He is. And as we are going to see later on, the Holy Spirit is also the Lord. How come, though? Do we believe in three Lords? Are there three gods? Do we believe in three gods? God forbid! Of course not. Yes, but then how do we say that each of the three persons is the Lord?

This is one of the mysteries of the truths of our faith. These truths are not discovered or invented or imagined by man. They are truths that were revealed by God Himself, through His Son and in the Holy Spirit. Then, how exactly could we explain this fact?

Each person of the Holy Trinity is not one third of the Holy Trinity. The mystery of divinity is not subject to mathematics and neither is it subject to pure and plain logic or reason. This does not mean that our faith is against reason and therefore illogical. God forbid! Our faith is simply above reason. The idea of God is neither logical nor illogical. It absolutely exceeds and supersedes logic. That is why Man was not able to reach the true God through any of his

The Creed

faculties. It was impossible for him to do so. That is why God had to reveal Himself to Man in order that he might know the true God.

However, we would like to know how there could be three persons and each one of them be the Lord. This, let us say, is 'achieved' by the fact that each one of the three persons is God Himself and not one third of Him. That is: when we are referring to the Father we refer to the whole of God and the same applies with the other two persons. When we are talking about the Son of God, we refer to Him as God and the same applies with the Holy Spirit. That is why we say *Jesus Christ, our God*. And that is why when we pray to the Holy Spirit and say: 'Heavenly King, Paraclete, Spirit of Truth', we pray to God as a whole and not to the one third of divinity. That is why we say *Lord* every time that we refer to each one of the three persons of the Holy Trinity. And, of course, each one of them is **one** and not more. And there cannot be any confusion among the three of them. They are three absolutely different persons. Each one of them has a different role and function in the divinity. They are not the same person who appears in a different way each time, as some heretics say.

And who is this second person of the Holy Trinity? It is the one that we refer to in the Creed next:

Jesus Christ

Jesus. This name comes from the Hebrew name *Jeshua* which comes from the older form *Joshua*. It was a common name amongst the Jews. This was actually the name of the successor of Moses. What does this name mean? It means *Saviour*. Literally, it means '*God saves*'. It was the name that the archangel Gabriel mentions to Mary: 'You have found favour with God: and behold, you will conceive in your womb and bring forth a Son, and you shall call His name Jesus' (Luke 1.31). And the same name was mentioned to Joseph by the angel: 'She will bring forth a Son, and you shall call His name Jesus, for He will save His people from their sins' (Matt. 1.21). He was also called Jesus at the time of His birth and also at his circumcision. The fact that the name *Jesus* means *saviour* in a typical and also in an essential way, is evident from the fact that Matthew (1.23) says: 'and they shall call His name Emmanuel', which means 'God is with us'. The two names Emmanuel and Jesus actually indicate the same idea. The child of Mary, conceived in her womb with the work of the Holy Spirit, is the Son of God, the Saviour of the world. This is 'achieved' by the fact that God, the Son of the Father, takes upon himself our humanity as well. This was necessary for us to be united with God, and in this way with Life Itself. In this way, salvation is 'achieved'. Therefore, the name *Jesus* expresses His divine-human nature. That is one of the reasons why Jesus calls Himself 'the Son of Man': in order to denote His 'added' human nature. In this way, He meant to stress the fact of His humility. Although He is God, the creator of the world, He takes on human flesh and becomes the 'seed of a woman' and becomes the Perfect Man that man ought to be. So the Perfect God also becomes the Perfect Man, God and Man in the same person, so that man could take up His divine nature and thus be saved.

Of course, Jesus is mainly called 'The Son of God'. That is what prevails in the New Testament. That expresses His divinity which distinguishes Him from His humanity. This is not absolutely connected with His birth, which is a work of the Holy Spirit, or even with His being the Messiah. Naturally, this is also meant. However, the prevailing idea is His relation with the Father.

Before we go on to that, which we are going to deal with in a little, let us deal with His other name: **Christ**.

Most of the times, we refer to Him with both these names: **Jesus Christ**. One who has never heard of Him might think that these are names of two different persons. However, they are names of the same person, as the two natures, the divine and the human, are also natures of the same person. Yet the two names have nothing to do with the notion of the two natures and the person of Jesus Christ.

What does **Christ** mean? It means *the Anointed One*. The idea of Messiah and the person of Christ meet together to identify Jesus who has always been Anointed by His Father as the Highest Prophet, the Archpriest and the supreme King. In many ways, *Christ* means *Messiah*. In this capacity, yes, Jesus was the fulfilment of all the prophecies concerning the expected Saviour of the nation of

Israel. Yet, the New Israel, the new nation, is finally proven to be all humanity that receives the salvation that is offered by Jesus and become members of His Body.

We could talk for hours about **Jesus Christ**. What we know well and we would like to stress here is that His name is the name above and beyond all names. It is not only because it is the most frequently uttered name, but it is the name that virtually works wonders and miracles. When His name is said in absolute faith, there is no doubt whatsoever that what we ask for will be granted to us. He Himself said: 'And whatever you ask in my name, I will do, that the Father may be glorified in the Son' (John 14.13).

the only-begotten Son of God,

begotten

When we say **begotten**, naturally we do not mean that He was born in the way that we are aware of. There is no relation between the birth that we know and this heavenly reality. There is not even any relation between this reality and His conception in the womb of the Virgin Mary and His birth therefrom.

The second person of the Holy Trinity is begotten from the Father in a completely unknown and mysterious fashion. The other thing that should be mentioned here is that this happens outside time. Since this is the case, we might as well say that the Son of the Father was always there. There was no time that the Son of the

Father did not exist. This is very clear in the Bible. Even in the Old Testament this is evident. However, this is absolutely clear in the New Testament. In the first chapter of his gospel, St. John tells us that the Logos or the Word in the beginning was there and that He was with God and He was God Himself (1.1).

the only-begotten Son

In Matthew (11.27) we hear Jesus Himself saying: 'All things have been delivered to Me by My Father: and no one knows the Son except the Father. Nor does anyone know the Father except the Son, and the one to whom the Son wills to reveal Him.'

The Bible, especially the New Testament, is very clear. In his Gospel, St. John says: 'For God so loved the world that He gave His only begotten Son, that whoever believes in Him should not perish, but have everlasting life'(3.16). And even more clearly: 'But Jesus answered them, "My Father has been working until now, and I have been working". Therefore the Jews sought all the more to kill Him, because He not only broke the Sabbath, but also said that God was His Father, making Himself equal with God. Then Jesus answered and said to them, "Verily, verily I say to you, the Son can do nothing of Himself, but what He sees the Father do; for whatever He does, the Son also does in like manner. For the Father loves the Son, and shows Him all things that He Himself does; and He will show Him greater works than these, that you may marvel. For as the

Father raises the dead and gives life to them, even so the Son gives life to whom He will. For the Father judges no one, but has committed all judgment to the Son, that all should honour the Son just as they honour the Father. He who does not honour the Son, does not honour the Father who sent Him. Verily, verily, I say to you, he who hears My word, and believes in Him who sent Me has everlasting life, and shall not come into judgment, but has passed from death into life. Verily, verily, I say to you, the hour is coming, and now is, when the dead will hear the voice of the Son of God; and those who hear will live. For as the Father has life in Himself, so He has granted the Son to have life in Himself, and has given Him authority to execute judgment also, because He is the Son of man. Do not marvel at this; for the hour is coming in which all who are in the graves will hear His voice and come forth – those who have done good, to the resurrection of life, and those who have done evil, to the resurrection of condemnation. I can of Myself do nothing. As I hear, I judge; and My judgment is righteous, because I do not seek My own will but the will of the Father who sent Me' (John 5.17-30). Jesus also says: 'I and My Father are one' (John 10.30) and also: 'Let not your heart be troubled; you believe in God, believe also in Me' (John 14.1), 'And now, O Father, glorify Me together with Yourself, with the glory which I had with You before the world was' (John 17.5) and 'Believe Me that I am in the Father and the Father in Me' (John 14.11). And St. Paul says: 'For in Him (Jesus) dwells all the fullness of the Godhead bodily' (Col. 2.9) and 'Looking for the blessed hope and glorious appearing of our great God and Saviour Jesus Christ' (Tit. 2.13).

begotten from the Father before all ages

Here we have the same word again: **begotten**. It is repeated after a few words. Why is this word repeated? To stress the fact that we mentioned above: that He is not made like all creation, both visible and invisible, material and immaterial. Everything and everybody was created. The Son of the Father is uncreated. He is **begotten**. He is begotten from the Father. He comes out of the same essence as that of the Father. That is why He has the same substance, as the Creed says here, in the same article. That is, He has the same nature as the Father. That is why He is God Himself. And when was He begotten from the Father? Was He begotten in time? Of course not. He would be a created being and even a material creation as well, if He were begotten in time. Was He then begotten in eternity? He was not even begotten in eternity. He would belong to the spiritual world then. He would just be a most brilliant angel. Therefore, He was not begotten even in eternity? When was He then begotten from the Father? He was begotten before all ages. In other words, He was begotten outside any connotation of time, not even in eternity, because eternity is not absolutely foreign to time. Eternity is just where time stops existing. Therefore, it is related to time, no matter how negatively. However, God is outside any sense of time. He is everlasting.

It is within this framework of the Father's Everlastingness, that the Son is begotten from the Father.

Light from Light

God is the Supreme Light, the real Light. The Light that God is is not comprehensible by us. The reason is that we have no experience of what true Light is. The experience of light that we have is not related to the true Light that God is. Conversely, the light that we know of makes it difficult for us to know the true Light.

Anyway, the true Light has a completely different nature than the light that we know of. And first of all, it is not material; it is spiritual. It is a spiritual reality. We might also say that it is a basic quality, or one might even more precisely say, that the true Light constitutes the substance of the Existence. According to this, God is the first Light; angel is the second light, very much related to the first Light, and man is the third light.

The Son is the first Light. How? We know that God is the First Light. The answer is given by what follows:

true God from true God

He is the first Light because he is true God. Yet, one might ask: 'How is it that the Son is the First Light since the Father is the First Light?' We said above that the Son of God is true God from true God.

Therefore, whatever the Father is, the same is the Son. Therefore, He is the First Light like the Father. And so is the Holy Spirit. The three Persons share the same divine attributes because the three of them share the same divinity. As there is not more than one divinity, the three Persons share the same attributes of God. Each person, when considered individually, is God in God's entirety. Each one is the entire God and the three of them is also the entire God. That is why we cannot discriminate among the three Persons. We cannot say that this Person is greater than the other. They are equal. Even that is not a statement sufficient to describe the relation among the three persons. They are not just equal, but they are, when individually considered, each one of Them true God. When we speak of the Father, we speak about the whole of God and the same happens when we speak about the Son and the same when we speak about the Holy Spirit. Of course, we should not misunderstand things. Each one of them is not just a kind of manifestation of the same God. That is: we do not believe that they are not really three Persons, but just one. Our faith in the existence of the three Persons is not arbitrary. Even the word *from* shows this fact. We believe that the Son of God is true God FROM true God. The Son comes **from** the Father. He is not the same as the Father. He is a different Person. If He were the same, then we would not say that He is true God **from** true God. As the Father is true God, so is the Son. This word, that is: the word **from,** was used twice above: begotten **from** the Father, Light **from** Light. The triple use of **from** is not circumstantial. It bears great significance. Firstly, it gives us the significance of the fact that the Son comes straight from the Father and secondly it tells us that the Son is another Person.

begotten not made

Again we come across this fact: that the second Person of the Holy Trinity is **begotten**. In other words, the Creed wants us never to forget this fact: He is **begotten**. And then it tells us that He is **not made**. He is not made like all the other creation, even the angels. Everything was created or made. This is not the case with the Son. He is **begotten**. And what does this mean? This is explained by the following words of the creed:

consubstantial with the Father

The word **begotten,** which we came across above twice, means that the Son comes out of the Father's substance or essence. What does substance or essence mean?

Everything has its own essence or substance. This substance or essence characterizes each creature or even each thing. Each one is identified with it. A bird cannot be a bird if it does not have the basic characteristics of a bird. Even a stone cannot be a stone if it does not have the basic features of a stone. Sponges and other similar sea life are not considered to be plants basically because they move and a plant is not supposed to be in motion. Therefore, they are considered to belong to the animal kingdom. Mushrooms do not belong to either realm, animal or plant, because they do not have absolute animal or plant traits. That is why they are considered to make up their own realm, that of fungi. We would need a lot of time and space to refer to all the cases that would reinforce our stand. However, let us come to man alone. Each man has his/her own characteristics. According to modern Biology there is a different DNA for each one of us. And modern Biology can establish whether my son is truly my son or not. If they examine his DNA, they would be able to find certain details which would prove, beyond any doubt, one of the two: his being my son or not. If the first applies, I might as well say that my son comes straight from me. He has the same substance with me.

It is true that the above statement is a very risky comparison. However, what else can we really say in order to establish, to a certain extent, the truth of the Son's being **begotten** from the Father? He is **not made** in the fashion that the whole creation was made. The table that I constructed, as a carpenter that I am, is not of the same substance like myself. It was made by me but it does not have the same nature like me. And this is so because it did not come out of my substance.

About the same, but, of course, in a mysterious and unknown manner, the Son was **begotten**, that is: He came out of the same substance of the Father. And like my son is a human being and not an animal, so the Son of God, is God as Himself. My son is a different person, yet he is man like me. The Son of God is a different person, yet He is God like His Father.

through Him all things were made

St. John says in his gospel (1.3): 'All things were made through Him, and without Him nothing was made that was made'. St. John stresses the fact that all things were made through Him. He says: 'and without Him, nothing was made that was made'. That is: all creation, both spiritual and material was made through Him. This means that all angels and in general all celestial creation and all the universe and everything that was made, Man included, was made through Him.

At first glance, this seems to contradict the things said in the first article of the Creed. There we said that the Father is the maker of all things visible and invisible, the heaven and the earth. Then what is true? Is it the Father that made everything or the Son?

To answer this question, we must refer to the role of each person. The will belongs to the Father. The will for the creation of anything that was created does not belong to the Son but to the Father. The Son wills nothing outside His own person. The Son only executes whatever the Father wills. He executes the creation of the spiritual as well as the material world. He also carries out the plan of the Father for the salvation of man. He does nothing against the will of the Father. Even the thought of such a thing is out of the question. He does not even go along and do things that are not in the will of the Father. And not only does He not go against the will of His Father but He obeys the will of His Father to the last word. One might say that one of the main attributes of the Son is the execution of the will of His Father.

Even in the Old Testament, one can find, in a rather concealed fashion, the existence of the Son. In Genesis, we read: 'And God **said**, Let there be light, and there was light'. Behind the word **said**, one can sense the existence of the Son of God. The Son of God, the One who took up human nature to save humanity, is actually the Logos, the Word of God.

It is not co-incidental that both Genesis and St. John's gospel start with the same phrase: 'In the beginning'. This phrase means: 'when time was still not there'. In the first lines of St. John's gospel, it is made absolutely clear that the Word of God was the creator of everything and everyone, and that this Logos or Word of God is Jesus who, though God, takes up human nature as well. This *kenotic* reality tells us a lot about the substance of God, and in this case of the Logos, the Son of God: that He is absolute humility.

Therefore, what do we learn about the first two persons of the Holy Trinity? We learn that the Father wills and His Word, the Logos, His Son, proceeds and does whatever His Father wills. Therefore, yes, the Father is the creator of all things, yet through His Word, His Son. Without His Word, the Father would not create anything. Of course, the world would be created because the Father wanted it to be created. In conclusion, the Father is the maker of everything, yet through His Son. However, the Son cannot say: 'I am the creator of all things.' He would not be able to create anything if His Father did not want to. And He would not take up human nature and be the Saviour of mankind if His Father did not send Him.

Article 3

For our sake and for our salvation he came down from heaven, and was incarnate from the Holy Spirit and the Virgin Mary and became man.

✝

For our sake and for our salvation he came down from heaven

For our sake

When you do something for the sake of someone, it naturally and basically means that you love and favour that someone. Therefore, a great love is here involved. It is not the kind of love that we are aware of. It is a kind of love that exceeds our power of comprehension. It is a kind of love that we have never and can never experience ourselves for anyone whatsoever.

As we mentioned above, He is our creator. Perhaps one could trace there the depths, grandeur and absoluteness of this love. One loves something that one makes. Yet this is not just somebody; it is God Himself. And the object of His love, in this case, is not merely something; it is Man. In the case of Man, God did not proceed to Man's creation in the same fashion that He did with the rest of creation. In the case of all other creation, He spoke and they were made. In the case of Man, he used other means for Man's creation. The Bible gives us the picture of God's using all His 'creative art' in order to create Man. And last of all, He breathed a gust of life into him. This gust of life is what makes Man a member of the spiritual world along with his partaking in the material world. Even his partaking in the material world does not make him absolutely equivalent to all other animals. Man's superiority is evident in every aspect of life in the world. And his superiority is not only due to his partaking in the spiritual world but to many other factors, from his bodily structure up to the most sophisticated features of Man's existence in this world. To say the least, Man is the only creature that draws a dynamic course of existence. All other animals draw a very static one. Man 'writes' History and creates civilizations.

We could speak for hours concerning this. However, it is not so necessary when every and each one of us bears witness to that fact. We know, deep inside us, that we are not mere animals. We are something much greater. We are, according to what has been revealed to us, the most precious creation of God; and even more specifically, of the Logos, of the Son of the Father. Each one of us was created in such a way that has more worth than the whole universe.

At the same time, though, we should never forget that this supreme excellence of ours is not due to us; we did not create ourselves. We owe everything, even our mere existence, to Him. It was for our sake that He does whatever He does and what is going to follow in the Creed, as well.

When we speak of the *sake*, we actually refer to the grace of God. What is this grace, though? Grace is the actual presence of the Holy Spirit. God's presence is made through the Holy Spirit. We shall see that later in the analysis, when we are going to deal with the eighth article of the Creed, which refers to the Third Person of the Holy Trinity.

The Holy Spirit is always present with the Logos, the Second Person of the Holy Trinity. It is not only during the baptism of Jesus that the Holy Spirit was present with Him, but It was always. And the same applies with the Father. It was not only when the Father's voice was heard, during the baptism of Jesus, but the Father is always present with the Logos. There is no case that the Three Persons of the Holy Trinity being divided or even separated. The incarnation of the Logos does not mean that a separation of the Logos from the other Two Persons takes place. The phenomenon of their common presence during Jesus' baptism does not mean an instant unity. The unity is everlasting.

The fact of the permanent presence of the Holy Spirit with the Logos is made evident from Luke's: 'And the Child grew and became strong in spirit, filled with wisdom; and the **grace of God was upon Him**' (Luke 2.40) and from John: 'And the Word (Logos) became flesh and dwelt among us, and we beheld His glory, the glory as of the only begotten of the Father, **full of grace and truth'** (John 1.14).

However, the grace of God, that is: the Holy Spirit, is always present in His Church. In the Acts, we read: 'And with great power the apostles gave witness to the resurrection of the Lord Jesus. And great grace was upon them all' (4.33).

and for our salvation

However, before the Creed says what God does for us, it says that, besides doing what He does for our sake, He does it for our salvation.

What is this *salvation*, though? We know that one is our saviour when one saves our life. I was caught in a fire in my house and a fireman came into my house and took me out of there. I was drowning and somebody came and drew me out of the sea and saved me from drowning. What kind of salvation is that that Jesus offers us? Well, the fireman and the life-guard at the sea, saved my life temporarily. That is: later on, after many years, perhaps because I was very old and my time had come, I had a natural death or I had a fatal accident at some time. There is nobody and there can be nobody who can save us from death once and for all. The only One that could do that is our Creator. And He did save us from death, the real death, which is separation from God who is Life Itself. The hymn for the Resurrection says that very clearly: 'Christ has risen from the dead, by death he has trampled on death and to those in graves given life'. And another

The Creed

hymn says: 'Though you descended into a tomb, O Immortal, yet you destroyed the power of Hell; and you arose as victor, O Christ God, calling to the Myrrh-bearing women: rejoice! and giving peace to your Apostles, O you who grant resurrection to the fallen'.

Jesus is crucified and dies on the Cross and is buried. However, on the third day He rises from the dead. With His death He defeats death itself. How does He manage that? When He dies on the Cross, Hades is obliged to accept Him. Yes, but Hades is the 'kingdom' of death and darkness.

We have a problem here. We know that God is the creator of everything. He must be the creator of Hades as well, then. Why did He create it? There is a major fallacy in the above statement and consequently to the question that follows it. God is not the creator of Hades. Then, one might say, God is not the creator of everything. Hades is not one of His creations. It is true that God is the creator of everything, yet He is not the creator of Hades. How can these statements stand, logically?

God created everything. Everything that exists is His creation. And this is due to the fact that He is Existence Itself. How then is He not the creator of Hades and if this is the case, who is the creator of Hades?

The answer to the above question is that God created all things that really exist: everything positively existing. In Mathematics there is a term which is called minus -. Minus - exists. We use it in Mathematics very often. But how does it exist? If someone has

The Creed

three apples and we 'give' him minus - three apples, how many will he have now? He will have none. And if we 'give' him minus - four apples, now he will not only have none but he will owe one. Correspondingly, the existence of Hades and of all evil is in the negative; that is: it has no positive existence. It is absence or even deprivation of any good. Therefore, evil is not a king; it is the catastrophe of any notion of any kingdom. There is death, but we must conceive it as an absence of life or the opposite of life. There is darkness but as absolute absence of light. Where there is light, there cannot be any darkness.

What do we mean by **salvation**? He saved us from Sin. This is the usual answer that one hears. However, what is Sin? Most people believe that sin or better sins are those actions or thoughts or utterances of ours that are against the will of God.

Let us see whether this is so. Sin is not a simple act against the will of God. By the way, what is the will of God? Some people say that sins are those things that give us a lot of pleasure. And they wonder why God is so much against the pleasant life (dolce vita, as the Italians call it and as it is internationally well-known) that we might choose to live. Therefore, there are many who stay away from God and His Church, because of that. They like that kind of life, they say, but the Church is against it. So why bother, they say.

One might wonder 'what is the writer trying to say? Is he perhaps in favour of dolce vita?' Well, there is no such intention on the part of the writer; on the contrary. On the other hand, he believes that the notion that most people have about sin is absolutely wrong. They take the results of Sin as Sin itself.

What is Sin, then? Sin is the separation of man from God. God does never send anybody away. How is then Man found to be away from God? Is it Man's choice? No matter how strange this might sound, the answer to the above question is 'yes'. Man chose to be away from God. There must have been a reason. Everything that occurs has a certain cause. So why did Man choose to be away from God? Of course, we know the story that is given in Genesis, about Eve having been persuaded by the devil to pick and eat one of the prohibited fruit of the forbidden tree. But the story in Genesis tells us that Adam and Eve were actually chased out of paradise. It was not a matter of their choice. What is the truth, then? Here we have two versions completely contradicting each other.

The answer to the above question is difficult and easy at the same time. It is difficult to prove to someone that no matter how binding the Bible is for our faith, it nevertheless sometimes conceals the real truth behind its words. We know, for instance, that behind the word 'said', the existence of the Logos, the Son of the Father, is concealed. For this reason, it is easy to answer the above question. It is easy because of the fact that God has revealed Himself in Jesus Christ. From this revelation, we know certain attributes of God that make it apparent that God never chases away anybody. On the contrary, God is ready to welcome anybody that wishes to approach Him.

Now, we come back to the above question: why should anybody want to go away from God? Why should Man want to go away from Him?

We know that God, among other attributes of His, is simple, plain, modest, humble. When Man was like God, simple and humble, Man was most happy in His company. When conceit entered Man's heart, then God was not the same as He used to be for Man. God was now different, because Man became different; Man was not humble any longer. God did not suit Man's 'taste'. Why can't the Jews accept Jesus? The answer is that they cannot accept a God that is crucified. They cannot accept the supreme humility that He is. In the minds of the Jews and of all those who are like them, God is the supreme pride, the supreme wealth, the supreme power. Of course, God is omnipotent, but His power is not of the kind that the Jews and most Men know. That is why these people will never be able to approach God; not because He does not want them but because they do not want God. God is too humble for them to accept.

Most people would pass by a poor fellow who is begging for their help, in a most scornful fashion. That poor fellow is nobody else but God. They disdain even to look at the poor fellow. They feel that they would stoop or lower themselves when they would condescend to even look at people of such base social standards. That is about the case with Man in relation to God. Some people have very wrong ideas about God when we speak of His glory, for instance. They forget that the glory of God is not merely different from the glory that they know of, but it is **the glory of humility**. That is one of the misinterpretations that many people have had of God. That is one of the reasons why, for instance, that the higher clergy are dressed in such glorious fashions. One would think, if one did not know, that our bishops are some kind of kings or even emperors, the way they are dressed, especially when they are supposed to praise Him Who is Humility. If, all of a sudden, He were to appear among them, not only would they not recognize Him, but they would have Him thrown out immediately; and who knows how many times this might have happened.

Above, we mentioned that the crucified and entombed Jesus descended into Hades. We established that Hades was not the creation of God. Anyway, Hades is not a place. Hades exists outside time and space. There is not a certain space that is allotted to it. Hades is a condition; the condition of absence of God or even a condition opposite to the one where God is present. Hades is the realm of death, which is absence of Life; of darkness, which is absence of Light; of anxiety and confusion, which is the absence of peace and tranquility. Jesus tells us that the Kingdom of God does not exist anywhere else but in us: 'the kingdom of God is within you' (Luke, 17.21), he tells us. In the same way, Hades exists there where there is no kingdom of God; in the hearts of people with a lot of conceit which brings about anxiety and confusion and all of their 'relatives'. In Hades, there is no Life, no Light, no peace; in fact nothing that is positive. Jesus Christ, the incarnate Son of the Father, dies on the

Cross, and Hades is obliged to accept Him. Satan, the 'creator' of Hades finds this as his greatest victory against God, whom he hates most because he is all conceit and God is absolute Humility. He thinks that conceit, death and darkness finally win over Humility, Life and Light Itself. He forgets that where there is Light darkness is defeated; where there is Life, death is defeated; where there is peace, confusion and anxiety are over. With the 'entrance' of Jesus, that is Light Itself, the 'kingdom' of darkness is destroyed. A hymn praising the Resurrection of Jesus says: 'When you descended into death, O immortal Life, then you slew Hades with the lightning flash of your Godhead'. This hymn is very strong. It depicts Jesus going down into Hades, as if it were a vast underground place and with an 'atomic bomb' He exploded all of it; He rendered Hades into dust. The explosion was so great that even the Heavens were shaken; this combined with the fact of His Resurrection. So another hymn says: 'Let everything in heaven rejoice, let everything on earth be glad, for the Lord has shown strength with his arm; by death he has trampled on death'. If we do **not** feel, down in the depths of our heart, the fact that a whole world of evil has gone to pieces and if it still seems to exist, yet that it won't last for long; it will not be long before it no longer exists; then we have not realized what has happened with the descent of Jesus into Hades and with His Resurrection which is actually our resurrection.

Jesus saves us from our conceit. With conceit, we can never approach God; not because He does not want us but because our

The Creed

conceit hinders us from approaching Humility Itself, that is God. Therefore, salvation is ultimately our freedom from conceit. When we are free from it, we can then approach God immediately. The supreme Humility draws our humility to Itself. And in the simplicity of both there is a spiritual union of God with Man: a union of Humility with humility, Plainness with plainness, Simplicity with simplicity. Conceit separates us from God and then we are lost. We are lost because we are separated from our creator; we are separated even from one another. All conceited people feel that they are self-sufficient. This makes them feel independent; they believe that they do not need anybody's help. This makes them create walls round their *ego*. This creates a profound estrangement not only from God but from all other people and even from Nature itself. Finally, this creates fear of others and everything; and ultimately, it creates hatred. When you fear someone, that someone finally becomes your enemy; and what you feel about an enemy is sheer hatred. And feelings of hatred most surely lead to acts of hatred. These acts of hatred are of numerous kinds: plotting against your enemy, beating him, hurting him, both physically and mentally, and worst of all waging war against him.

The History of Man is filled with wars carried out between the nations. Actually, at times, History seems to be a mere story of the wars that the various nations of the world waged against each other. It is actually the result of the separation of Man from God. And this separation was 'achieved' by nothing else but conceit.

In the parable of the prodigal son, the younger son develops conceit within his inner self. He believes that now he has grown enough not to need the protection and love of his father. That makes him believe that he can manage by himself. If what he was only interested in was his father's property, he would perhaps get it but stay with his father. However, the moment he achieves his aim of getting the property, he leaves. He feels that he does not need his father for his life any longer. On the contrary, he does not feel comfortable in his presence.

In our case, God does not wait for us to ask Him to give us what we want. He gives us even more than what we would perhaps ask for. However, as in the case of the prodigal son, he does not demand that we stay with Him. He does not send us away. He does not want to get rid of us as some parents of today do. On the contrary, He very much wishes that we remain close to Him. What happens, though, is that once we realize what we have in our hands, we forget that everything was given to us by Him; and we try to use all that in the ways that we want and not according to His plan. This leads us to the tragedy which is called War. And the reason for that is that what was given to us seems like fire, which can be used constructively but it can be used destructively as well, when the one who has it in his hands does not use it in the way the giver of the fire knows. The latter happened in the case of Man.

The cause of the turn of Man towards his catastrophe is the fact that Man was given freedom by God. One might superficially say that the fall of Man and therefore his sin is a consequence of his freedom. The same person might say that therefore, freedom of will should not have been given to Man. However, this means that God made an error and a very grave one, too. However, we realize that this is unacceptable. How could God make a mistake? He would not be God, then. Error cannot be part of the essence of God. On the contrary, absolute perfection is one of the fundamental attributes of God. However, the problem remains unsolved. And first of all, we must be absolutely positive whether freedom is the real cause of the fall of Man or not. That is: should we blame freedom for that? The answer to this question is a dual paradox: yes and no. We have to blame freedom for the fall of Man. If Man had no free will, then Man would never have fallen; even if Eve and Adam did the same; even if he or she stretched his/her arm and picked the same forbidden fruit. There would be no case of God's even telling them not to eat it. What purpose would that serve? None! Therefore, the fall took place because Man was free to do it or not to do it; because he had free choice. Man was not created with a mere instinct. If he were, then he would not have had free will and, therefore, he would have never fallen. We are now positive that it was the attribute of Man's freedom that made it 'possible' for him to sin and fall. However, freedom is not to be blamed for that. We referred to fire above. The same applies here. When you are given fire, you can use it well, for your benefit, but you can use it wrongly and bring about a calamity. The matches in the hands of a child's parents that are useful are yet dangerous in the hands of their young children. Again, one might think that God made a mistake by giving free will to a still immature Man. God should have waited until Man was mature enough to know how to use it. Again, we have to stress the fact that God never makes mistakes. God created Man in His image and likeness. Man could never be Man from the beginning if he had not had freedom from the beginning. Man was not created in order to sin but in order to remain eternally or even 'ever-lastingly' close to God. However, he had the choice of going away from God. If he did not have that choice, then his freedom would not be real. God, being omniscient, knew of the fall before it happened. That does not mean that He should not have given Man free will. The fact that He knew it does not mean that God should have stopped His plan of creating Man. When we say such things in this way, we think of God as if He were one of us. God's knowledge of the fall of Man before it happened, served not in the canceling of the creation of Man (which is an unacceptable thought) but in planning Man's salvation.

Sometimes we call it redemption. However, a redeemer gives money to a kidnapper or a slave-driver in order to set a hostage or a slave free. How could we think of Jesus' blood in the hands of the devil, though? And we must never forget that the devil is not as powerful as we think. And the devil is not as wise or even clever as we think. He is sinister and sly but he is powerless and stupid. He was such an idiot that he did not realize what that plan of God was for our salvation. His malice was so great that rendered him blind and dumb.

he came down from heaven

he came down

Another difficulty with human language. **He came down**; from where? The answer that is readily given: **from heaven.** Therefore, here we think of heaven as somewhere up high and that we are at a lower level; and He comes down from up there to down here. We should never take these words or phrases literally. If we do, we are in heresy. The literal interpretation of these phrases depicts God as moving. However, God is not supposed to be in any kind of motion. Motion needs space in which it takes place. Space means confinement. God is not confined. God would not be God if He were confined. Therefore, God should never be supposed as being in space, because He is never supposed to be moving. And, of course, whatever His coming down means, this should never be taken as a change of position. We are, of course, only aware of movement meaning a change of position in space. 'I moved' means that I was at a point A and now I am at a point B. This is not the case with the coming down of the Logos. Many, if not the overwhelming majority of Christians (including the Orthodox), not only think but believe that the Son of God was absent from heaven for thirty-three years that is, during his stay on earth. However, this is utterly unacceptable. How could we think of the Son of God, that is God Himself, in terms of space as we would think of any sheer human being? One might ask: 'how then should we think of it?' We should think of God as omnipresent. The same applies with the Logos. He was here on earth but at the same time He was in heaven as well. 'And what about His ascension?' one might ask. 'How did He ascend up to heaven, if He were always there?' The answer to this question will be given below when we are going to deal with His ascension. For the present, we should be reminded that ascension, resurrection, crucifixion and in general all of the events of Jesus' life refer to us.

The phrase *He came down* is a most significant one. This phrase means the end of religion. Religion was and is characterized by the great physical, mental and spiritual struggle of Man to 'ascend' spiritually as high as possible in order to reach Man's Creator. Therefore, in the case of religion we have an obvious attempt to ascend towards heaven. In the case of the Logos, we have God Himself descending to earth. It is apparently the exact reverse direction. God shows Man that Man does not need any longer to try to ascend in order to reach the Creator.

Jesus' birth marks the end of religion. The case of the Magi is not coincidental. The Magi from the East represent the religions of the earth coming with reverence to kiss the newly-born baby which is the Saviour of the world: the Logos Who was made flesh in order to extinguish all distance between Man and God. Man could never reach God by going up in any way: either in an arrogant way, as in the case of the Tower of Babel, or with prayers or the other great ways that religions tried. His birth in a stable shows the way to effectively approach Him; and not only approach Him but be united with Him. It is something that the peoples of the various religions must be informed of. We are not allowed to leave them in ignorance of the gospel, which is nothing else but the good tidings that the shepherds heard from the angels in the night of Jesus' birth: 'do not be afraid, for behold, I bring you good tidings of great joy which will be to all people. **For there is born to you this day in the city of David a Saviour, Who is Christ the Lord.'** (Luke 2.10-11). The above reference has a lot of messages to give us. The first is **do not be afraid**. Fear is one of the factors on which religion is based. And it is one of the reasons why sometimes our faith, too, is turned into religion, which is inexcusable. The message that is given with the birth of Jesus is that Man need not feel any fear in Man's relation with God. Of course, we sometimes use the phrase *fear of God*. Yet this is not the fear that we know. It is the great and overwhelming reverence or awe that we feel before the supreme humility that He is. It is His humility that we 'fear' and not Him. We 'fear' His humility because we can never reach its heights. Our heavenly Father is much more lovable and approachable than our earthly father. The angel gives the reason why they should not fear. The word *for* prepares us to hear the reason. The word *behold* draws our attention to the greatest of all messages that has ever been given; *the good tidings*, as the angel says. The good tidings are not merely good. They are *of great* *joy*; we might as well say the greatest bliss that Man has ever experienced: the taste of heavenly pleasure. And this message and this exultation is addressed *to all people*. No one is excluded. And the message itself is: **For there is born to you this day in the city of David a Saviour, Who is Christ the Lord.'** For your sake, for the sake of all the peoples of the world; *this day*: that is, two thousand years ago, which, though, applies to all ages; *in the city of David*: that is, in a particular place which was designed before all ages and which was prophesied by the prophets; *a Saviour is born*. Instead of the indefinite article ***a***, there should actually be the definite article ***the***. There is no other Saviour. The Saviour is One and He is the incarnate God, ***Christ the Lord.***

The Logos' coming down means something else as well. It means the splitting of Man's History into two. We usually think of the shape of the Cross as casual and as having no importance. Yet it has great significance. The Cross has two lines: the one parallel to the ground, the earth, and the other perpendicular to it. The parallel line denotes the course of time. Time does not draw a circular course, as the Ancient Greeks (except Hesiod) believed it did. We believe that Time draws a straight line. And because of that, it has a beginning and an end. That is why we have protology and eschatology, whereas the Ancient Greeks did not. It is not a coincidence that the Bible starts with the phrase *In the Beginning*. This is how the Old Testament starts. And if the New Testament began with the gospel according to St. John, it would start with exactly the same phrase: *In the beginning*. This is the protology of our Theology. And it is not a coincidence that the last book of the Bible, the book of the Revelation, is a book that relates the last days and the end of the earth and the universe in general and the beginning of a new world, the Kingdom of God.

We could go on saying so many things about the horizontal line of the Cross. Yet, our main interest here is the perpendicular one. This line cuts the other line into two. This is the great intervention of God into Man's History in order to save Man. This line denotes the coming of God down to earth and the end of religion. At the same time, if we look at it the other way, the reverse one, we can see what happens with those who are crucified there on the Cross together with Jesus (like St. Paul) and accept the downward coming of His for the salvation of the human kind. Their destiny is Heaven. That line, the perpendicular line, now with an upward impetus, takes them to heaven instantly or it could also be a course of a whole life depending on the plan that God has for every and each one of us.

Consequently, we might as well say that, through the Logos, Who comes down to earth, we are taken up to Heaven and we become citizens and inheritors of the Kingdom of God.

from heaven

The word **from** is a preposition which denotes the origin. Finally, someone arrives somewhere. Let us say that the place of arrival is point B. If someone asked him where he had been before he went there, he would give the place of his origin. Let us say that the point of his departure was A. So, the person was at point A and he moved from there and came to point B. This is how things of this world of ours work. You cannot find yourself somewhere, at some point B, if you had not been at a certain point, let us say A, before you began your journey towards point B.

However, things do not function in the same fashion with heavenly matters. The Logos was in Heaven before He came down to earth. And it is from there, Heaven, that he came. We all know that He did not fly from there to down here. He did not cover that distance in any way that we would know of. This is related to His incarnation, to which we shall refer a little later. And the vehicle is none known to us. The 'vehicle' was the Holy Spirit. And there is something else here: there is no movement in this case. In this world of ours, the notion of *from* cannot be comprehended without the existence of motion. However, here there is no motion. Again, motion is inapplicable to God. We must repeat here that God can never be thought of as moving. Movement means change and change brings about wear and ultimately the consequence of wear is death. Yet, God cannot be conceived as changing, and therefore He can never be thought of as being worn and, of course, God never dies. The realities of change, wear and death, that are so natural for earthly existence, have no relation to God. Even the thought of any of these being related to God is revoltingly outrageous.

The Creed

As it was mentioned above, God is omnipresent. Most religions, even our faith, when it becomes a religion, think of God as transcendental. That is, they think of God as not belonging to this world, but to a world that is beyond this one. According to them, in order for one to reach God one has to make a very great leap: from this world, the world of sensation, to that one, the supernatural world of eternity where God is found.

It is true that God is not confined in space, any space. However, if we say that He is absent from space, then we are contradicting ourselves. His omnipresence means that He is in space as well. Therefore, God, yes, is outside space but He is in space as well. Of course, He is not confined in space. However, if we say that, for that exact reason, He is not found in space, it is as if we are saying that He is confined outside space. That is: the exclusion of God from space, is some kind of confinement. And, anyway, it means that He is not present in space. However, if He is not present in space, He is not omnipresent. The conclusion is that God is outside space but He is in space as well. He is not confined in space but, at the same time, He is present in space as well. That is, He is *there* (out of space) but *here* (in space) as well. To make things as simple as possible: God is omnipresent through His Holy Spirit, the Third Person of the Holy Trinity that makes this possible. It is not coincidental that it is in the prayer to the Holy Spirit that we say: 'Heavenly King, Paraclete, Spirit of Truth, **present everywhere, filling all things**'. This prayer tells us that the Third Person of the Holy Trinity is the Heavenly

The Creed

King, He is the Spirit of Truth, He is present everywhere and that He is filling all things. The last two qualities are actually answering our problem. He is present everywhere and He is filling all things. The last quality, that is: filling all things, actually emphasizes the first: everywhere present. There is no place where He is not present. The most remote place, the tiniest of things or particles actually cry out and say: 'Here He is!', and that **He** is none other than the Holy Spirit. Therefore, He is in Heaven, which is why we say *heavenly King*; He is also in space and time as well, which is why we say: 'filling all things'. And this is the plain truth, which is why we say: 'the Spirit of Truth'. And we call Him Spirit, because we cannot see Him; but then, exactly because He is Spirit He is everywhere, as the air is (about) everywhere. However, He is even more undiscovered than the air or a gust of wind. You can feel the wind or the air with your senses; yet, you cannot do likewise with the Holy Spirit, except in a spiritual way. One of these ways is prayer. Prayer is not just the words that we utter while praying. Sometimes words are said without our mind being close to Him to Whom we are supposed to be speaking. A prayer is a conversation of our spirit with God, and most particularly with the Holy Spirit. The spirit that was breathed into us during our creation into what we are, that is: human beings, speaks to the Spirit that made us Men. The spirit that is in us speaks to its originator: the Holy Spirit. That is what prayer is. This conversation is not necessarily made up of words as the conversation that we know of. This conversation is mental, spiritual and even better

The Creed

it is a conversation of the heart of Man with the Spirit of Truth and Love, which is the Third Person of the Holy Trinity.

From Heaven. What is this Heaven? Many people believe that Heaven is the sky. In Greek, the word for sky and heaven is the same: ***ουρανός*** *(ouranos)*. There was and there still is such belief among people. Especially in the past, people used to look up towards the sky and believe that God was up there; there, where Man could not reach Him. It was this idea of inaccessibility that made Men think of God as residing there, in the sky. It was this belief that made men of ancient times start building the tower of Babel so that they might reach the sky and high up there be able to reach God and in this way not have any fear of Him and thus be able to defy Him. The Ancient Greeks even thought that their gods resided on the summit of Mount Olympus which was inaccessible and the highest point of the land of Greece. The conception of transcendence is linked with the notion of inaccessibility. We now know that they were wrong but for them that was a fact. Of course, one wonders how the Greeks, with all that curiosity that characterizes them, did not attempt to climb up there and see their gods. The only possible answer to the question must be that they did not try it out of reverence.

What do we Christians believe about Heaven? Heaven is the Kingdom of God, which is not in space or a kind of space itself. As we said before, the fact of something or someone being in space is mere confinement. Therefore, God is outside any idea of space, being omnipresent. However, let us say in simple terms, His right 'domicile' is Heaven: that is a condition in which there is no confinement whatsoever.

Therefore, the Son of the Father came *down* from heaven. *Down* to where? The answer: down to earth, of course. What do we mean by *down*? As we mentioned above, for God there is not any idea of space. However, the idea of *down* denotes a movement from somewhere up high downwards to a lower space. The notion of downward movement here is of a spiritual rather than material character. God condescends to take up flesh, something completely foreign to His Nature. He also chooses to become one of His creations, Man. He is conceived in the womb of a woman, the Virgin Mary; He is born in a family, He is under the Mosaic law and under all the laws, social and natural, that every Man is under. And all that, in order for Him to save Man. St. Paul, in his epistle to the Galatians, says: "But when the fullness of the time had come, God sent forth His Son, born of a woman, born under the law, to redeem those who were under the law, that we might receive the adoption as sons. And because you are sons, God has sent forth the Spirit of His Son into your hearts, crying out, 'Abba, Father!' Therefore you are no longer a slave but a son, and if a son, then an heir of God through Christ' (Gal. 4.4-7).

There is another question concerning the downward movement of the Son of the Father, as was mentioned above: Was the Son absent from Heaven while He was down here, on earth? Human reason would say: 'yes, of course, He was absent from Heaven while He was down here'. And the same person who would answer in this way might also refer to the fact of Jesus' ascent up to Heaven. In order for one to go up, one must have been down or at a lower level before. One might further argue that no one can be down and up at the same time. This would be a violation of the principal laws of Physics.

All of the above are absolutely logical. No thinking person would argue against such reasoning. However, here we are not dealing with a common person. We are dealing with the Son of God, the creator of the world and all of its laws. The Creator cannot be subject to His creation and its laws. He is above and beyond them. Therefore, while Jesus was on earth, He was in Heaven as well. However, there is something that cannot be explained. We know that Jesus, after His ascension up to Heaven, sat at the right hand of the Father. This seems to mean that He had not been there before. He did sit next to the Father. This again is a kind of thinking that is linked with existence in space. And there is something else: all the events of Jesus' life are closely related to Man. The Son of God did not need to become Man. He was born on this planet in order for Man to be reborn in a new kind of life. He lived on earth so that Man would live in Heaven. He was crucified so that Man would crucify his own old self. He was buried in order for Man to bury his old self and all of his sins. He went further down into Hades in order to free Man from Hades. He was resurrected in order for Man to be resurrected into the New Creation. He ascended into Heaven so that Man would ascend up there as well. He sat to the right hand of the Father so that Man would do likewise. Or, we might say that

Jesus' ascension into Heaven and His sitting at the right hand of the Father, was made for the sake of Man. The Son was always there; the new event is that Man, in the person of the incarnate Son of God, ascends and sits there as well. Of course, the sitting at the right hand of the Father, might be a prize for the Son for His absolute obedience to the Father. There was just 'hesitation' on the part of the Son: when He begged His Father: "O my Father, if it be possible, let this cup pass from me". That, however, shows exactly the opposite: the struggle He made (in His human nature) to overcome the supreme difficulty of sacrificing His life. We all know how life is the supreme good that we possess. Without it, nothing has any value or worth. Jesus (always in His human nature) 'is asked' by His Father to sacrifice this supreme good for the life of the world'. This is the vital part of God's plan for the salvation of Man. His plan is that the Son sacrifices Himself. This Sacrifice which first takes place during the Last Supper, actually takes place on the Cross. This same Supreme Sacrifice continues to take place, in a different fashion unknown to us, up in Heaven in the Heavenly Altar. In the Holy Liturgy, during the preparation for the Holy Communion, the deacon (or the priest) says: 'For the precious gifts here set forth and sanctified, let us pray to the Lord. That our God who has accepted them in His Holy and immaterial Altar above in Heaven as a saviour of spiritual fragrance, may send down upon us in return his divine grace and the gift of the Holy Spirit, let us pray.' Up there, in Heaven, another kind of Sacrifice takes place all the time. There, the archpriest who sacrifices is Jesus. According to St. Paul, as Jesus was from the tribe of Judas, which, according to the Mosaic law, was not a priestly tribe, He was not supposed to be a priest. However, Melchizedec, the king of Salem and priest of the most high God, was a priest long before the Jews had a temple and therefore they had no priests. In this way, Melchizedec was another kind of priest. Melchizedec here plays the role of the image of Jesus who was going to be archpriest of another kind: after the order of Melchizedec and not after the law of a carnal commandment, but after the power of an endless life (Hebrews 7.17). All that is in accordance with Psalm 110,4: 'you are a priest for ever according to the order of Melchizedec'. The main fact is that, up there, in the Heavenly Altar, Jesus Christ is the unique archpriest who, in eternity, offers Himself as a Sacrifice for the salvation of Man. The uniqueness is found in the fact that here we have the sacrificer (the offerer of the sacrifice) and the object of sacrifice being the same. This is one of the mysteries concerning our salvation. How could the one who sacrifices and the one who is being sacrificed be the same? Perhaps the answer is found in the creation of Man: 'And the Lord formed man of the dust of the ground, and breathed into his nostrils the breath of life; and man became a living soul' (Gen. 2.7). This is one of the most significant lines of the whole Bible. If we focus our attention on this line, we might find the answers to many questions. One of the answers might be the one we are seeking. The breath of life that is described here as being breathed in (through the nostrils of Man) is nothing else but

Life Itself. And it is this Life that man lost with his fall. The Life that is nobody else but the Logos, Man's creator. Therefore, now the Logos that, in this case, is Jesus Christ, the incarnate Son of God, is both the Saviour of the world and Man for whom He is willing to be sacrificed. Perhaps it is here that we are supposed to focus our attention to the mystery of how the one who sacrifices is the same as the one who is being sacrificed. The living soul, which is Life itself, is sacrificed for Man who is also Him Who is concealed in Man. And there is something which should be considered: the unity between God and Man. The Three persons of the Holy Trinity are united with each other into One Divinity. The great multitude of human persons are supposed to be united among them into one humanity. Humanity is actually united with the Holy Trinity through the Second Person, the Saviour of humanity, in the Third Person, the Holy Spirit, with the Father, the source of Divinity. This reality of unity answers the question 'how could the one who sacrifices be the same as the one who is being sacrificed?' For the Holy Trinity, it does not matter (the way we think it matters), which one of the Three Persons is being sacrificed. Of course, it is the Second Person who is being sacrificed. However, this sacrifice cannot be thought of as solely affecting just this one Person, the Second Person. The whole of the Trinity 'suffers'. It is inconceivable for just one Person of the Holy Trinity to be 'suffering' and not the other two, as if they were strangers to the Second Person. It is impossible to think that the Father is so far distant from His Son when He is on the Cross. Jesus' cry on the

Cross: 'Eli, Eli, lama sabachthani? that is, My God, My God, why have You forsaken Me?'(Matt. 27.46) does not refer to the distance that existed (even at that moment) between the Father and His Son (which, as we saw and shall see, never existed, even throughout the Son's being on earth). The cry refers to Man's distance from God throughout all Man's History away from God, because of Man's willing fall. In this supreme cry, Man realizes the tragedy of tragedies of his fall. Man finally acknowledges that his existence cannot be away from his creator. Now, at last, Man is ready to return to Him who created him. The separation from Him has lasted too long for him. It is as if he is saying: 'How could I, Oh God, be away from you for so long? In a little, I will be surrendering (together with your Son) this kind of life of alienation, on this Cross and I will be returning to you, together with your Son. I shall be resurrected with Him from the grave and my Hades of existence in death and I shall be ascending together with Him into Heaven, and I will be sitting together with Him at your right hand.'

Finally, we must be as clear as possible about the Son's descent to the earth. We must know that His descent does not mean the descent that we know of. It does not mean that after His descent He ceased to be in Heaven for as long as He was on earth. He continued to be there as well as here on earth. Actually, he continued to be everywhere, as God. 'If this is so,' one would ask, ' then why is the Bible using this word?' The answer is that first of all human language, as in all these occasions, finds itself unable to describe transcendental experiences. The word *descent* describes the humiliation that God suffers to appear Himself here on earth. The real *descent* is better described with the words that follow:

and was incarnate from the Holy Spirit and the Virgin Mary and became man.

and was incarnate

and. This word denotes the continuation of the work of God, especially concerning the salvation of Man. He **was incarnate** denotes what 'happened' to the Second Person of the Holy Trinity in order for the plan for the salvation of Man to be fulfilled. The word *incarnation* comes from the Latin word *caro, carnis* which means *flesh*. In other words, **was incarnate** means that He took **flesh** upon Himself. He took upon Himself something which was foreign to His nature as God. Flesh is a material thing and He is pure Spirit, the purest. In this way, He was mingled with something that was extremely inferior and foreign to His nature and essence. This is the first time that we come across this attribute of God: simplicity. In this case, we have God in His greatest *kenosis*. What is *kenosis*? It is a Greek word *κένωσις* meaning the act of emptying. What kind of emptying is this, though? St. Paul says: 'Who (Jesus), being in the form of God, did not consider it robbery to be equal with God, but made Himself of no reputation, taking the form of a bond-servant, and coming in the likeness of men. And being found in appearance as a man, He humbled Himself and became obedient to the point of death, even the death of the cross' (Phil.2.6-8). As we have above, there is no limit to God's humility. Imagine, the One who can pose for everything, since He is everything, is the most simple and humble of all.

It is worth mentioning here the circumstances in which St. Paul says what we have just quoted. St. Paul writes to the Philippians and says: 'Therefore if there is any consolation in Christ, if any comfort of love, if any fellowship of the Spirit, if any affection and mercy, fulfill my joy by being like-minded, having the same love, being of one accord, of one mind. Let nothing be done through selfish ambition or conceit, but in lowliness of mind let each esteem others better than himself. Let each of you look out not only for his own interersts, but also for the interests of others. Let this mind be in you which was also in Christ Jesus'(Phil. 2.1-5). And then St. Paul continues to say what we quoted above. In this way, we are now sure that God shows us the way to Heaven: through Humility and only through that.

from the Holy Spirit

from. This usually denotes the origin or where something or someone comes from. In this case we are stating what it was that made the incarnation of the Son possible. And the answer is given immediately afterwards: **the Holy Spirit**. This was made possible with the action of the Holy Spirit.

Some people, even Christians, even 'Orthodox' Christians, show an inexcusable doubt or even disbelief about the incarnation of the Son of God. They forget that this is the basis of our faith. If you doubt or even disbelieve this fact, then you are not a Christian. It is as simple as that.

The reason that they do not believe it is that it is against natural laws. They forget that the laws were set by God and He is the only one who can, at any time, supersede these laws. One might argue that He is supposed to be the first to be consistent to these laws because He was the one that set them. This is not the case here, though. The laws were set by God so that there might be harmony and order in the universe. He is the only one who knows how to deal with them because He is the founder of the Universe and its laws. He does not violate them at every instance but only when the order, the real order of the universe, is shaken. In this case, the greatest of orders was shaken: the order of the relation between the crown of His creation, that is Man, and Himself were disturbed; not only disturbed but mixed up altogether.

There is something else: God is omnipotent. There is nothing that He cannot do. Therefore, why is there such doubt or disbelief about such a serious matter as the salvation of Man?

and the Virgin Mary

The word **and** usually adds something to something else. In this case, it adds to the fact that the incarnation took place with the action of the Holy Spirit. The other factor that contributed to the incarnation of the Son of God is **the Virgin Mary.** Who is **Mary,** Maria or Mariam or Miriam? In the Hebrew language, it is actually Mir-yam, which means *rebellion*. And it is truly a name of rebellion. The rebellion here is related, among other things, to the other name, actually a feature of Mary, which is **Virgin**. How could she be a mother and a virgin at the same time? This is something that makes some people doubt or even show disbelief about the incarnation of the Son of God. It is in fact very difficult or even impossible for a woman to be pregnant and at the same time be a virgin. We have parthenogenesis in the case of certain plants, insects or even animals but not in humans. In the case of Maria, there is still another 'revolution' against nature: the fact that even after the birth of Jesus, she remained a virgin. Everything about the birth of Jesus is 'revolutionary'. It could not be otherwise. Here we have the birth of Jesus who is the Son of God, the Logos, through Whom all were created. Why should one wonder about that when He was the one who created everything from absolute nothing? If He were able to do that, why could He not also be born in the way we believe He was? There is nothing that is impossible for God.

There is, however, another question that needs to be answered concerning the birth of Jesus by a virgin: 'why should He be born in that way and not in the way that everyone is conceived and born?' Let us suppose that He were born in the normal way; what would that mean? It would mean that He would not be in the least different from us. He would be a mere man; not God at the same time. He would not bear both natures: divine and human. This would mean that not only would He not be able to save us, but He would need salvation Himself. Why is that so? Let us suppose that He were born like us; that would mean that He would bear the same nature as ours: the fallen nature of Man; He would have the stigma of our fall. This would mean, as was mentioned above, that He would have to be redeemed like us. He would be in the same turbulent sea as us and He would need someone from outside to come and save Him along with us. That is where the answer is found: *outside the turbulent sea.* He had to be from a source outside the condition that we were in. The only possible outside source was the divinity. That is why the saviour of Man, Jesus Christ, the Son of God, had to be born in a different way. The only way was the one that we know: **from the Holy Spirit and the Virgin Mary.**

First of all, how is the Spirit involved here? Why should it be from the Holy Spirit? Why could it not be from God in general? The reason is that God is not a vague idea; He is a very concrete Being, and He is three persons. 'Why then', one might argue, 'did the three persons not act in unison?' The answer is: 'how could they act in unison when one of the three persons was supposed to be born?' One can understand very well that the Second Person could not be the actor of the birth of Jesus; He was the one that was to be born. 'Why then', one might argue again, 'not the Father?' The answer to this question is very simple: each one of the three persons has a certain 'function' within the Holy Trinity: to the Father, the Will is attributed; to the Son the execution of the Will of the Father; and to the Holy Spirit, the giving of meaning, life and purpose is attributed. From what we can gather from the above, the birth of Jesus could only be the work of the Holy Spirit and of no other person of the Holy Trinity.

Now we come to the question: 'Why should there be a woman involved? Could God not give birth to Jesus without the involvement of a woman? Is He not omnipotent?' Of course, He is omnipotent but He is also most benevolent. He gave Man His image, which, among other attributes, means that Man was created to have free will. Therefore, his salvation should go along with Man's freedom. The abolition of freedom for Man would mean that He would not be the image of God any longer. God would never abolish this attribute of Man because He is most benevolent, as mentioned above. That is the reason why the Son of God, the saviour of the world, had to be 'born of a woman, born under the law, to redeem those who were under the law, that we might receive the adoption as sons' (Gal. 4.4-5).

Now, we come to another question: 'why should this woman be a virgin?' We know that God does not pour scorn on the weakness of Man. We gather that from the fact that Jesus was so understanding towards even the common women and towards Man in general. He stresses the fact that He came to save the fallen Man, the sinner and not the righteous. Why then was He not born from any woman? Why should He be born from a virgin? There are many reasons. One of them is that His birth was not to be a common birth but a birth from the Holy Spirit. Another reason is that the woman who would be chosen for this role, the Mother of God, was to be an exceptional one. One of the exceptional qualities was that she should be willing to accept this role. A virgin of the kind of Mary was ready to accept this unique role because, among other things, she was virgin and humble. The purity of her soul and body made her humble enough to accept the calling of God Himself. And the most significant words ever uttered from a human mouth in the history of the human kind, were her answer to the archangel Gabriel: 'Behold the maidservant of the Lord! Let it be to me according to your word' (Luke 1.38).

How do we know that the conception of Jesus in the womb of Mary was the work of the Holy Spirit? St. Luke, the evangelist, is very explicit about it. The angel's answer to Mary's question: 'How can this be, since I do not know a man?' (Luke 1.34) was: 'The Holy Spirit will come upon you, and the power of the Highest will overshadow you; therefore, also, that Holy One who is to be born will be called the Son of God' (Luke 1.35). What else do we need to know? The description of the conception is so precise. No more words are needed to describe it.

and became man.

The work of the Holy Spirit was to make the Son of God into Man. Does the word 'became' mean a change, a transformation from God to Man? God forbid! It means that He also took upon Himself the nature of Man along with His divine nature. With His birth Jesus is both God and Man at the same time, in the same and unique person. That is: now we have two natures in the same person. The creed is very clear about that; 'He became Man'. It does not say He appeared to be Man when in fact He was only God. He did not make us think that He was Man. He was truly Man like us. St. John, the evangelist, the beloved disciple of Christ, says very explicitly: 'And the Word became made flesh, and dwelt among us, and we beheld His glory, the glory as of the only begotten of the Father' (John 1.14). The Fourth Ecumenical Synod stresses this fact beyond any doubt: Jesus Christ is the incarnate Son of God, both God and Man in the same One and unique person.

Article 4

He was crucified also for us under Pontius Pilate, and suffered and was buried;

✝

He was crucified

The fact that, after the article about our Lord's incarnation, the Creed brings us to His crucifixion is significant. It is as if it says that that was the purpose of His incarnation: to be crucified. This might sound very strange to some ears. How could it be so? The centre of His whole work on earth is focused on His crucifixion and His resurrection. Without these, His incarnation would have no meaning at all. Why is that so?

There were a lot of theories about the above issue. One of them was that someone had to pay for Man's Sin. This was undertaken by the Son of God Himself. This theory was founded and developed in the West. The reason for this is that the West and especially the Romans see things in a very legalistic manner. In this scenario, they see God as a Grand Judge who sits up there on His throne with His books of His own Laws open, judging everybody according to those laws. And even worse than that, those laws are not much different from human laws. Those western theologians imagine God turning the pages of those law books of His every so often to see what His own laws say about this and that and act accordingly. He Himself is not allowed to act in any other way but that; which is similar, if not the same, to that of a common judge here on earth.

According to this theory, Man committed a great Sin, one of disobedience against God. After that, God opened His books of His laws and read: 'in such a case, Man should be chased out of Paradise' and that was what happened: Man was thrown out of paradise. Now, God, in His benevolence, decides to give Man another chance. But how could that be? There is no other way but through His Son. His Son will become a Man and He will be crucified and, in this way, He will pay (as a Man, a representative of the fallen Man in general) for all Men. In this way, Man is redeemed of His Sin and now Man can return to where he was before, and God's justice is satisfied.

That is the way the western theory sees the whole work of Jesus, the Son of God, on earth. It seems a logical theory. A lot of Christians, even great theologians believed in it and made it their own. However, is this theory correct or wrong? Let us examine it.

First of all, God is not the kind of judge that these people believe He is. Of course, He is just. He is not only just, but He is justice, real justice, itself. However, we should never forget that above that, He is Love. We can see that in the parable of the prodigal son. When the prodigal son comes home, the father does not question him. He does not judge him. He does not set up a court and carry out a session of justice, with Him as the judge trying to decide whether it would be legal (that is: according to the laws, His laws) to accept His son back into His mansion. On the contrary, when His son kneels before Him in great repentance, He holds him up and gives orders to His servants to serve him and prepare a grand feast to celebrate His son's return. Therefore, we can see here that His love is superior to His justice. From the above parable, we also learn that even above love, God is freedom. We can see that from the fact that He does not prevent His son from going away from Him. He does not intervene in any way or use any means, direct or indirect, to force him to come back to Him. He lets him decide for himself. Finally, the son decides to come back to Him willingly and with great zest.

There is also something else which is very important concerning the attributes of God. We mentioned that He is justice but that above that He is love, and even above that He is freedom. We should notice, however, that above even that, He is simplicity. Without this simplicity, the three Persons would not be one God. The simplicity or plainness is expressed in His humility, His *tapenosis*, His *kenosis*. In the case of the crucifixion, this simplicity takes the form of self-abnegation and self-abasement for the sake of Man. What do we mean by that, though? We mean that everything that Jesus does or says is for the sake of Man. The greatest of all, though, is the example that He gives for Man to follow. And this example is that of utter humility. His most humble birth in a stable, His life in a humble home of a poor carpenter, His public life when He had nowhere to stay, His passion, but most of all His death on the Cross, show us the way: the way of humility. He never poses as someone important and that is what we are supposed to do: to be humble as He is. It is the only way to approach God; it is the only way to be united with God and be saved.

There is also something else that has to be said about the Cross. There is actually nothing coincidental in the Bible; everything in it has a certain manifest or hidden meaning. One of the most significant items of the Bible is the Cross. In addition to the well known significance of it, its shape has another great meaning as well. The bar which is horizontal to the ground (on which Jesus' hands were nailed) is the line representing the course of time and history. The Christian aspect of time is that of the straight line. It is not that of a circle which was the aspect of the Ancient Greeks (except Hesiod, who had the same aspect like ours). Our aspect of the straight line provides us with the fact that time has a beginning and therefore, it has an end as well. That is why we have protology (relating to the beginning of this world) and eschatology (relating to the *eschata*, that is: the end of this world). The circle has no beginning point and no end. That is why the Ancient Greeks did not have any protology or eschatology. They believed that the same events happen again and again at a sequence of the completion of the circle of

The Creed

time which, according to them, had a certain duration. This line also means that the History of Man, which has a beginning, will have an end, which will coincide with the end of the universe. According to the creed that we are dealing with, Jesus Christ will come again. This second time, He will not come in the humble way that He did the first time but it will be in great glory, in all of His glory, which is unimaginable. This second time He will not come to save Man but to judge Man. He will judge us, the living and the dead. And from then onwards, the only Kingdom that will exist is His Kingdom which will have no end. This second coming of His, will be combined with the resurrection of the dead; and His Kingdom will be combined with the life of the age to come, which is the true Life.

The other part of the Cross, the bar which is perpendicular to the ground, is like a line cutting the other line (the horizontal one) into two. This line represents the first coming of God into our world in the person of Jesus. While the horizontal line represents the history of man as well, the perpendicular line (that is the first coming of God into the world) cuts the history of man into two: the history before and the history after Jesus Christ. This perpendicular line means the powerful entrance of God into our world in order to save the world from its fall and destruction. It comes down from Heaven and it even enters the ground and goes deep into it. This represents the entombment of Jesus. The whole of our world, on the surface, in the air and deep inside the ground must be remedied and saved. However, the perpendicular line has still another meaning. It goes from deep in the ground upwards and points to heaven. It shows us where we should have our eyes turned to: towards Heaven. Real Christians live down here on earth but they behave as if they were heavenly citizens. It also shows our destiny, which is Heaven, the Kingdom of God. It shows us where Christ has ascended and where He 'sat', that is: at the right hand of the Father. It tells us that our destiny is there.

He was crucified also for us

also. This word means the following: He was not only incarnate, which was too much for us, but he was also crucified for us.
for us, that is: for our sake. This phrase was used above as well. Everything that Jesus did was for our sake. He took up human nature for our sake and He was crucified for our sake, that is: in order that we might be saved by being united with True Life which is Him.

This phrase also means something else as well. It means that, by being crucified, He indicated the way of salvation, that is: we are supposed to crucify ourselves, our old selves, in order for us to be resurrected along with Him. We should not expect any personal resurrection if there is not any personal crucifixion.

Most of the times, this personal crucifixion is referred to the crucifixion of our passions. We forget what passions really are. Passions are the dynamic part of our inner world. One might ask: 'Why then are we trying to fight them and uproot them and drive them out from our depths?' We forget that this is wrong and it is wrong because we are in ignorance of what passions really are. As we said above, passions are the dynamic part of our inner world. 'How, then,' one might ask, 'did they develop to become the way they are?' We usually use the word *passions* with a very negative connotation. However, we sometimes use the word *passion* in a positive way. We say, for instance: 'He did it with passion', that is: he did it with all of the might of his inner world. Passions are in fact that inner power with which God endowed us. With this power we are destined to reach up as high as possible and attain divinity. Why then, do we refer to passions with such contempt and with such disposition to fight against them and destroy them? The answer to this question is found in the reality of our fall. Together with our fall, everything in us fell and most of all: our inner power. Actually, it is this inner power that we used in order to fall. We used it in order to become gods outside the plan of God for our deification. The part of us that fell most, we might say, was this inner power of ours. It is this power that leads us to our sin and our catastrophe. Therefore, it is not the passions that we should fight against but this tendency of ours to want to become gods by violating the plan of God for our deification. Therefore, what we should fight against is not this power that is implanted in us but our pride and our selfishness which draws us down and away from God. "What should we do with our passions, then?' one might ask. We should not uproot them as most people say. When we 'manage' to do that, then we are going to be left without this power that God enriched us with. We should try and give them a different direction: instead of downwards, we should turn them upwards. If we manage to do that, and with great impetus, we have succeeded in our spiritual struggle for perfection.

Therefore, what is needed to be done is to fight against our selfishness, our conceit and egoism and not against our passions. If we manage to do that, then our inner power will lead us towards God. What we should sacrifice, then, is not our passions but our conceit. We could do that by following Jesus' example. We must be reborn in the cave of his humility; we must sacrifice our own will and our conceit and bury our old selves in order to be resurrected with Jesus into an entirely new life. To do that, we must first acknowledge our sinfulness. We must recognize our miserable spiritual state like the prodigal son and kneel before the Father. Whatever we are, whatever we manage to do in our life, we must think of it all as rubbish when all that we did was not for the glory of God. We must discover the truth of vanity of this world and that we are nothing without God. In other words, we must develop inside us this virtue of simplicity and humility without which, nothing can be achieved spiritually.

Therefore, our struggle for our salvation should be focused on this: the imitation of Christ's supreme humility on the Cross.

under Pontius Pilate

There were many that claimed that the person of Jesus and therefore everything about Him, and of course the event of His crucifixion, were a myth. For them, there was not really such a person as Jesus Christ. Well, the part of our creed refers all of them to a piece of very concrete evidence. One can very easily search and find that there was really this person: Pontius Pilate. In general, the Scriptures cannot be considered as a myth like many other books of various religions. The Bible is filled with documents of what it refers to. It gives so many genealogies. In fact, the beginning of the New Testament starts with a long genealogy. It is as if the Bible, and in this case the New Testament, said that what you are going to read here is not just the imagination of some writer or writers, but concrete truth, a kind of science. This means that our faith is metaphysical but at the same time it is science, a particular kind of science.

Who exactly was this Pontius Pilate? He was the procurator of the Roman Empire in Judea. He served as procurator for ten years (26-36 AD). He was appointed in 26 AD governor of Judea by the Roman Emperor Tiberius. These are historical facts which nobody can deny. Furthermore, the whole story that is given by the evangelists relating to Pontius Pilate is not easy to be rejected or characterized as a product of fantasy.

We could go on to describe the personality of Pontius Pilate and his role. However, we do not think that that has any relevance to our effort to analyze the Creed. Our main purpose here is to establish that the crucifixion is a historical fact.

and suffered

Jesus **suffered**. There is no doubt about that. The nails with which He was crucified pierced his flesh. The pain must have been most acute and severe. However, that was not the whole story: besides two other people, infamous criminals, were actually suffering the same bodily pain. However, Jesus' pain was much greater and of another kind at the same time.

During the Holy Week, we commemorate His Passion. His passion on the Cross reaches its climax; yet that was not all. His passion starts from the moment He knew that His disciple, Judas the Iscariot, was going to betray Him. From that moment onwards, His body was sacrificed for the world. He offers His precious Body and Blood to His disciples at the Last Supper. His passion had already started: the abandonment of His disciples at the critical time of His anticipation of His arrest at Gethsemane and all those things that were to happen; the agony in the garden of Gethsemane is His great ordeal. He Himself says: 'My soul is exceedingly sorrowful, even unto death' (Matt. 26.38). He is so agitated that He even prays to His Father: 'O my Father, if it be possible, let this cup pass from me' (Matt. 26. 39). He finds Himself being alone, deserted even by His disciples. Their eyes are so heavy that they go to sleep; human weakness proves invincible. They cannot stay awake and keep Him company during these terrible hours of expectation and agony. Then His arrestors arrive; Judas, His betrayer, along with them. Judas, His disciple, to whom He trusted their small fund for their sustenance, is there in front of Him. He approaches Him; he kisses Him, not out of love but as a sign of betrayal. The people to whom He was so benevolent all these years, giving them their health in a miraculous manner, whom He taught so divinely, now attack Him and arrest Him as if He were a criminal. And His disciples? What do His disciples do? Do they try to protect Him? Only one of them, just for a minute, tries to defend Him by cutting off one of the archpriest's men's ears. But then they leave, they abandon Him. Even worse, the gospel says: 'Then all His disciples **forsook Him**, and fled' (Matt. 26.56). Only Peter and John followed timidly. As the Bible says: 'But Peter followed Him afar off unto the high priest's palace, and went in, and sat with the servants to see the end' (Matt. 26.58). He followed Him to deny Him three times later on. At the third time 'he began to curse and to swear, saying, I do not know the man' (Matt. 26.72).

At Annas', of the high priest father-in-law's, before whom He was first taken, one of the officers there hit Him with the palm of his hand (John 18.22). From there, He was bound unto Caiaphas the high priest (John 18.24).

At Caiaphas', the archpriest's palace, false witnesses appeared accusing Him and He was condemned to death by Caiaphas and the people there. And they spat in His face and ridiculed and mocked

Him 'and buffeted Him; and others smote Him with the palms of their hands' (Matt. 26.67).

Finally, they decided to put Him to death. We are not to think that He took everything lightly. He must have suffered as everyone of us would have suffered. He now knew absolutely well (always in His human nature) that His death was a matter of time. The inner agony must have been unbearable. At the same time (in His divine nature, as the Son of God, the creator of everything and everyone), He must have suffered unimaginably from seeing His supreme creation (Man) in such a miserable state. In a way, He must have thought: 'how could Man, my chosen creation, have fallen so low! How could they put me, their creator, to death?'

Then they bound Him and 'led Him away, and delivered Him to Pontius Pilate, the governor' (Matt. 27.2). Before Pilate, He was accused by the chief priests and elders, the spiritual leaders of the people (His people). Man reached the climax of Man's injustice and false appreciation of real justice. Jesus was silent. The governor marveled at the fact that He did not say anything. Pilate did not find anything wrong with Him. He even tried to find a way of letting Him go free. He proposed to release Him or Barabbas, an infamous prisoner. He expected that they would prefer to have Jesus free instead of Barabbas, who was a dangerous criminal. 'But the chief priests and elders persuaded the multitude that they should ask for Barabbas, and destroy Jesus' (Matt.27.20). Jesus was there; he was listening. He could hear His creation preferring the release of a

The Creed

dangerous prisoner rather than His own. He heard His creation and particularly His chosen people shouting, demanding that He should be crucified. Then Jesus saw Pilate washing his hands. The same happens every time that politics face such realities; personal interest and the misinterpreted peace and order prevail in their judgement. A man (and that is what Jesus is for Pilate: a mere man) may as well be sacrificed, even an innocent one, for the interest of the rest and for the keeping of law (what law!) and order (what order!). The washing of his hands is considered by him as enough to make him feel that he is 'innocent of the blood of this just person' (Matt. 27.24). The fact that he believed that Jesus was innocent did not prevent him from scourging Him. Then Pilate's soldiers stripped Him of His clothes and put a scarlet robe on Him. They plaited a crown made of thorns and they put it on His head and they gave Him a reed to hold and they bowed their knees before Him' (Matt. 27.27-29), all in mockery, 'saying, Hail, King of the Jews! And they spat upon Him, and they took the reed, and they smote Him on the head. And after they had mocked Him, they took the robe from Him and put His own raiment on Him, and led Him away to crucify Him.' (Matt. 27.29-31).

For some distance, He carried His cross. It was after some time that the Roman soldiers assigned the job to one Simon, the Cyrenian. Therefore, for some time Jesus Himself was carrying the cross on which He was going to be crucified in a little.

When they reached Golgotha, which means a place of skulls, they stripped Him of His clothes and then He was crucified; that is:

He was nailed to the wood of the cross which was laid down to the ground. After that, His cross was raised. He was extremely thirsty because of such a long time not having a drop of water and because of the exhaustion and the loss of much blood with the nailing. He asked for water. And what did they give Him? They gave Him vinegar mingled with gall to drink. Here is what the gospel says: 'After this, Jesus knowing that all things were now accomplished, that the scripture might be fulfilled, said, I thirst! Now there was set a vessel full of vinegar: and they filled a sponge with vinegar, and put it upon hyssop, and put it to his mouth. When Jesus therefore had received the vinegar, he said, It is finished: and he bowed his head, and gave up the spirit' (John 19. 28-30).

He was crucified between two other men who were the worst kind of criminals. Actually this kind of death was only reserved for people of that kind. Jesus had this kind of extreme humiliation as well.

His greatest ordeal, though, is found in His desperate cry: 'Eli, Eli, lama sabachthani? that is to say, My God, my God, why hast thou forsaken me?' (Matt. 27.46) It was the worst moment of His passion. Up there on the cross, He feels that He is forsaken by everybody, even His Father. Therefore, we should never forget that He is the only one that gives comfort to all those who feel the same. Once He said: 'Come unto me, all ye that labour and are heavy laden, and I will give you rest' (Matt. 11.28). Of course, in order for that to be so, one should have in mind what Jesus Himself says: 'All things are delivered unto me of my Father: and no man knows the Son, but the

Father; neither knows any man the Father, save the Son, and he to whomsoever the Son will reveal him' (Matt. 11. 27).

There is no suffering, no pain, physical or inner anguish or passion, that Jesus did not go through; even this one of absolute abandonment, which we sometimes feel in our life. The only person who can give us consolation in such occasions is He who suffered the same to its climax, and who is able, as the Son of God, to help us. He is able to give us not only comfort but the greatest of company (His own) and at the same time He is able to turn our sense of abandonment into the greatest of blessings: closeness to God; the greatest that one could think of.

And last, and worst, of all, He suffered death: 'and He bowed His head, and gave up the spirit' (John 19.30). He who is Life Himself suffers this that is exactly the opposite of what He is: death. That is why the angel tells the myrrh-bearing women: 'Why seek ye the living among the dead?' (Luke 24.5).

and was buried

When He died on the cross, things did not finish, in many ways. Of course, before He gave up the spirit, He said: 'It is finished' (John 19.30). However, that means that the *Oikonomia* or dispensation for which He received our nature and *worked* for our salvation has now been completed. It had finished but not all of it; only a part of it: the part which was to be done on earth and while He was *wearing* the worn human flesh. Now this human flesh is done with and is ready to be buried. Yet, things did not prove so easy.

First of all, an unshaken proof should be there that He was really dead. 'Therefore, because it was the Preparation Day, that the bodies should not remain on the cross on the Sabbath, (for that Sabbath was a high day), the Jews asked Pilate that their legs might be broken, and that they might be taken away. Then the soldiers came and broke the legs of the first, and of the other who was crucified with Him. But when they came to Jesus, and saw that He was already dead, they did not break His legs. But one of the soldiers pierced His side with a spear, and immediately blood and water came there out.' (John 19.31-34). 'After this, Joseph of Arimathea, being a disciple of Jesus, but secretly, for fear of the Jews, asked Pilate that he might take away the body of Jesus; and Pilate gave him permission. So he came and took the body of Jesus. And Necodemus, who at the first came to Jesus by night, also came, bringing a mixture of myrrh and aloes, about a hundred pounds. Then they took the body of Jesus, and bound it in strips of linen with the spices, as the custom of the Jews is to bury. Now in that place where He was crucified there was a garden, and in the garden a new tomb in which no one had yet been laid. So there they laid Jesus, because of the Jews' Preparation Day, for the tomb was nearby' (John 19. 38-42).

The burial of Christ, even His actual death, is a most significant event in the work of our salvation. With His death and burial, Jesus enters the realm of Hades. Our Church calls this Jesus' descent into

Hades. The word *descent* betrays the reality of Death bringing Man down instead of up. It is actually the outcome of Man's fall. There is no other 'place' from Hades for Man to enter after Man's fall. It is the realm of Death which was already there because of the fall of the fallen angels. There are no other 'places' for Man but these two: God's Kingdom and Hades. The former is the one where all creation was placed by its creator; the latter is the 'place' where the fallen creation is found. The former is close to God; the latter is away from God. Therefore, the former is close to Life and every good; the latter is away from God and therefore away from Life Itself. Being away from Life is a state which is called death. In other words, death is absence of Life or more accurately: it is the opposite of Life. The former is the outcome of the will of Man (or even the Angels) to be close to their Creator; the latter is the outcome of the will of Man (or even the Angels) to be away from God.

The Church has a hymn which is a very strong depiction of what really happened with the descent of Jesus into Hades. The hymn goes: 'When you went down to death, O immortal Life, then you slew hell with the lightning flash of your Godhead!' Here the hymn depicts Jesus descending into Hades and slaughtering hell, which is the state in which Man is found before the work of Jesus' dispensation. Hell was the misery of the fallen Man. Why is this considered as past? Because now something tremendously great has happened. Jesus, as God, descends into Hades like a lightning flash or even bolt; one might even say a huge atomic bomb. Hades explodes. It

The Creed

is now in small pieces that soon disappear. Hades is dissolved. The icon depicting the Resurrection shows Jesus holding Adam and Eve by their hands and pulling them up from Hades which is now in pieces. We can also see the keys, with which Man was firmly and tightly bound and kept there by Man's previous master, the devil, now broken and thrown away. Naturally, that is true for all those who accept Jesus Christ as their Lord and are united with Him.

From the above, we realize how significant the descent of Jesus into Hades was and how this was one of the major parts of the dispensation. Jesus could not ignore those who had already departed from this world and had gone into their Hades. His work is catholic. This means, among other things, that it embraces all places, that is: it is universal and embraces all of time. The latter means that it embraces the past, the present and the future. His Church is also catholic in the same way. Therefore, this is one of the reasons that He had to die and be buried.

As every event of Jesus' life has a parallel significance for us, so is it in this case. Jesus is crucified for Man to crucify Man's old self. Man can crucify Man's old self only by self-denial like that of Jesus. Man has to humiliate himself in the way that Jesus humiliates Himself on the cross. St. Paul exclaims: 'Knowing this, that our old man was crucified with Him, that the body of sin might be done away with, that we should no longer be slaves of sin. For he who has died has been freed from sin. Now if we died with Christ, we believe that we shall also live with Him.' (Rom. 6.6-8). And also: 'I have been crucified with Christ; it is no longer I who live, but Christ lives in me; and the life which I now live in the flesh I live by faith in the Son of God, who loved me, and gave Himself for me' (Gal. 2.20).

Article 5

He rose again on the third day, in accordance with the scriptures,

✝

He rose

Jesus rose from the dead. The resurrection of Christ is a unique event not so much in relation to His life but more as a unique moment in Man's history. We must repeat here the fact that all of the events of Christ's life are always related to Man for whom He received human nature: in order to save him, which ultimately means reunion with the source of Life, which is God. Man was separated from God willingly. Now Man is given the time to be reunited with God and in this way with Life Itself. With Man's fall, being away from God and therefore away from Life, Man was in the 'area' of death. Now, with the resurrection of Jesus Christ, Man is resurrected along with Him. In this way, Man, along with Jesus, wins over death and is united with Life again. Before the resurrection, Man was in

Hades, a prisoner of death and of the founder of death (that is: separation from God, who is Life), Satan. Now Man wins over death in the person of the resurrected Jesus. Jesus is not resurrected for Himself. That is why His resurrection is our resurrection. That is why the Orthodox iconography of the resurrection does not say: THE RESURRECTION OF CHRIST; it says: THE RESURRECTION. And this is so, because, ultimately, the resurrection of Christ is not actually so much His but ours. Jesus Christ, as the Son of God, did not need either to die or to be resurrected. Anyway, as Life Itself, it was impossible for Him to remain in Hades. Therefore, the only reason that He was resurrected was for us to be resurrected from our death, that is: from our separation from God. Our resurrection does not happen instantly. It does not happen once but always; every time that Man accepts what is being offered from God through Jesus Christ: the Heavenly Lamb of God.

The *troparion (the hymn)* of the Resurrection is known to everybody: 'Christ is risen from the dead by stepping victoriously over death and in this way He granted Life to those who were in the graves'. Who were those that were in the graves? All of us. We know very well that it is only a matter of time before we are found there. And it is not only that. Our existence away from God is an existence which does not differ from that of those that are in graves. Those who are buried in graves are without any life in them; those who are away from God are virtually without any Life either. We chant the above *anastasimos* (relating to the resurrection) hymn very often on

The Creed

and after Easter day. This is not done by accident. Our Church wants us to know it by heart and we chant it so often so that we might be always conscious of its importance for our lives. Without it, our faith would be vain. St. Paul says: 'Now if Christ is preached that He has been raised from the dead, how do some among you say that there is no resurrection of the dead? But if there is no resurrection of the dead, then Christ is not risen. And if Christ is not risen, then our preaching is empty and your faith is also empty. Yes, and we are found false witnesses of God, because we have testified of God that He raised up Christ, whom He did not raise up - if in fact the dead do not rise. For if the dead do not rise, then Christ is not risen. And if Christ is not risen, your faith is futile; you are still in your sins! Then also those who have fallen asleep in Christ have perished. If in this life only we have hope in Christ, we are of all men the most pitiable. But now Christ is risen from the dead, and has become the first fruits of those who have fallen asleep. For since by man came death, by Man also came the resurrection of the dead. For as in Adam all die, even so in Christ all shall be made alive (I Cor. 15.12-22).

again

He rose **again**. Why *again*? This is not the second or third or more time that He rose. It was the first and the last. Therefore, the word *again* must be related to something else. As we mentioned above, Jesus' resurrection was actually the resurrection of Man. Before the fall, Man was close to God. Man was actually united with God. We know that the Son of God was in Man. Therefore Man was high up spiritually. His fall is the separation of Man from God and therefore from the Son of God. Therefore, with the resurrection of Jesus, we have the resurrection of Man. So Man is raised again to the high levels of divinity. During the Holy Oblation we pray and say: 'You brought us out of non existence into being, and when we had fallen you raised us up **again,** and you left nothing undone until you had brought us up to Heaven and you had granted us your Kingdom that is to come'.

on the third day

Christ died on the cross on Friday and was risen on early Sunday morning, that is: in three days' time. This was in accordance with the Scriptures. The Greek original text says: **'Τη μια των Σαββάτων'**, which means: 'On one of the Sabbaths'. Why does it say so? What is the meaning of it? It is clear from the context that the Jewish (derived from the Egyptian) twenty-four hour period of the day of Sabbath was over and the new day was dawning. The new day was considered as the first day of the week. It is for this reason that the English version is: 'Now on the first day of the week...' (John 20.1). That is why we celebrate Sunday as the day of Christ's resurrection and not on Saturday. That is why the Sabbath of the Jews becomes Sunday for us Christians, which in Greek is called **Κυριακή** (Kyriaki), which means the day of the Lord.

The Creed

Things might seem very simple; yet they are not. The Sabbath was the last day of the week and it still is. Saturday closes the cycle of the seven days of the week. And with Sunday a new week starts. However, this day (Sunday) is considered by many Church Fathers as the eighth day. Why? How could there be an eighth day in a seven-day week cycle? This is impossible, at least according to scientific or simple human standards. What is the meaning of the eighth day? It means that the Resurrection of Christ marks a new era in Man's History or even better in Man's destiny. First of all, it means that the idea of time is being transformed. This transformation of time is very important for our Church. Our Church actually 'moves' and acts within this framework of the eighth day. It is the beginning of our entrance into eternity. That is why we have this very significant feeling that time is not composed of past, present and future any longer. It is a perpetual present. That is why, for instance, we chant: 'Today Christ is being crucified'. We do not say that He was crucified two thousand years ago. This notion of 'today' is evident in all the practices of our Church. His Resurrection is happening now and His Ascension into Heaven and His sitting at the right hand of His Father and His glorious coming again is happening today, now. That is why there was and there still is (among true Christians) this certainty of His second coming soon. We have this sense, this certainty that He is among us all the time and the Holy Spirit and His Father as well. That is why we say 'to the Father, the Son and the Holy Spirit, now and for ever, and to the ages of ages' so often in our liturgical practice. That means that the Holy Trinity, as a whole but as individual persons as well, is present in our Church; and as a whole or as particular persons acts in it all the time. The word *now* gives exactly this idea of the sense that we experience eternity which is not divided into past, present and future. Eternity is actually a kind of eternal present and everlasting presence of the Holy Trinity. The phrase 'for ever, and to the ages of ages' means exactly that, that the past and the future are concentrated in the present and are dissolved in it. This is the so called transformation of time. It is not the same as what science calls deformation or distortion of time. The latter happens with the acceleration of speed and or with the increase of gravity. The division of time does not cease to exist in science. Philosophy considers it as not existing objectively but only psychologically. The latter is right; yet philosophy knows that time exists, and we measure it and it affects our lives. However, neither science nor philosophy can really tell us the significance of time and its purpose in our life. Our aspect of time is that of **ΕΥΚΑΙΡΙΑ**, which means OPPORTUNITY or CHANCE, which is composed of two parts: **ΕΥ** (= good or well) + **ΚΑΙΡΟΣ** (time). Therefore, time is granted to Man from God in order to grasp this opportunity or chance to be reunited with Christ (through the holy communion) and in this way be reunited with LIFE (God), from which Man was separated and found himself in the opposite state, that is: of death. Now there is only biological death which does not have the sting of the previous kind of death that had the poison of the permanent separation of Man from God. Now biological death does not affect Man negatively and neither is it a curse as it used to be; now death is the termination of the existence of Man in real death (separation of Man from God) and a blessing because it gives Man the new stage of Man's existence to live the real Life united with God.

in accordance with the Scriptures

St. John Chrysostom finds many traces of the resurrection in the Old Testament. One of them is the birth of Seth from Adam and Eve, after the murder of Abel by his brother Cain (Gen. 4.25). According to psalm 40 and 16, the resurrection is common for everybody; while the resurrection which is going to be in glory will be for those who have lived a just life. We also have pre-images of the resurrection with the transportation of Enoch into heaven without dying. St. Paul says: 'By faith Enoch was taken away so that he did not see death, and was not found, because God had taken him; for before he was taken he had this testimony, that he pleased God' (Heb. 11.5).

Another sign of the resurrection is that that the Old Testament relates about Elijah: 'And it came to pass, as they (Elijah and Elisha) still went on, and talked, that, behold, there appeared a chariot of fire, and horses of fire, and parted them both asunder; and Elijah went up by a whirlwind into heaven' (2 Kings 2.11). Psalm 118 says: 'I shall not die, but live, and declare the works of the Lord. The Lord hath chastened me severely, but He has not given me over to death'. (17-18).

At various places in the Old Testament we read: 'After two days will he revive us: in the third day he will raise us up, and we shall live in His sight' (Hosea 6.2). 'Yet it pleased the Lord to bruise Him; He hath put Him to grief: when thou shalt make His soul an offering for sin, He shall see His seed, He shall prolong His days, and the pleasure of the Lord shall prosper in His hand. He shall see of the travail of His soul, and shall be satisfied: by His knowledge shall my righteous servant justify many; for He shall bare their iniquities. Therefore will I divide Him a portion with the great, and He shall divide the spoil with the strong because He hath poured out His soul unto death: and He was numbered with the transgressors; and He bare the sin of many, and made intercession for the transgressors'. (Isaiah 53.10-12). 'And He will swallow up death in victory; and the Lord God will wipe away the tears from off all faces; (Isaiah 25.8). 'Thy dead men shall live, together with my dead body shall they arise. Awake and sing, ye that dwell in dust: for thy dew is as the dew of herbs, and the earth shall cast out the dead' (Isaiah 26.19). 'The hand of the Lord was upon me, and carried me out in the spirit of the Lord, and set me down in the midst of the valley which was full of bones. And caused me to pass by them round about: and behold, there were very many in the open valley; and, lo, they were very dry. And He said unto me, Son of man, can these bones live? And I answered, O Lord God, thou knowest. Again He said unto

The Creed

me, Prophesy upon these bones, and say unto them, O ye dry bones, hear the word of the Lord. This saith the Lord God unto these bones; Behold, I will cause breath to enter into you, and ye shall live; And I will lay sinews upon you, and will bring up flesh upon you, and cover you with skin, and put breath in you, and ye shall live; and ye shall know that I am the Lord. So I prophesied as I was commanded; and as I prophesied, there was a noise, and behold a shaking and the bones came together, bone to his bone. And when I beheld, lo, the sinews and the flesh came up upon them, and the skin covered them from above: but there was no breath in them. Then said he unto me, Prophesy unto the wind, prophesy, son of man, and say to the wind, Thus saith the Lord God; Come from the four winds, O breath, and breathe upon these slain, that they may live. So I prophesied as He commanded me, and the breath came into them, and they lived, and stood up upon their feet, an exceeding great army. Then He said unto me, Son of man, these bones are the whole house of Israel: behold, they say, Our bones are dried, and our hope is lost: we are cut off from our parts. Therefore, prophesy and say unto them, Thus saith the Lord God; Behold, O my people, I will open your graves, and cause you to come up out of your graves, and bring you into the land of Israel. And ye shall know that I am the Lord, when I have opened your graves, O my people, and brought you up out of your graves. And shall put my spirit in you, and ye shall live, and I shall place you in your own land: then shall ye know that I the Lord have spoken it, and performed it, saith the Lord' (Ezekiel 37.1-14).

The last prophecy can be easily traced as being realized in the New Testament: 'Then, behold, the veil of the temple was torn in two from top to bottom; and the earth quaked, and the rocks were split, and the graves were opened; and many bodies of the saints who have fallen asleep were raised; and coming out of the graves after His resurrection, they went into the holy city and appeared to many' (Matt. 27.51-53). Of course, that does not mean that this is the main significance of the prophecy. It mainly refers to the last articles of our Creed: 'I await the resurrection of the dead and the life of the age to come'.

Article 6

And ascended into heaven, and is seated at the right hand of the Father.

✝

And ascended into heaven

Before Jesus ascended into heaven, He appointed a certain mountain in Galilee for his eleven disciples to meet Him. He spoke to them and told them 'All authority has been given to Me in heaven and on earth. Go therefore, and make disciples of all the nations, baptizing them in the name of the Father and of the Son and of the Holy Spirit, teaching them to observe all things that I have commanded you; and, lo, I am with you always, even to the end of the age' (Matt. 28.18-20). 'Now it came to pass, while He blessed them, that He was parted from them, and carried up into heaven' (Luke 24.51).

Forty days after His Resurrection, Jesus ascended into heaven. What is the significance of it? Was there a need for Him to ascend up into heaven? Was He absent from Heaven all the time that He was down here on earth?

If we do not answer the above questions, there is going to be a gap in our faith. We must distinguish between the Son of God, the second person of the Holy Trinity, and the incarnate Son of God in the person of Jesus Christ; not that we are referring to two different persons. Our dogma is that the divinity and the humanity exist in the same person, Jesus Christ, the incarnate Son of God. Let us remember that the Son of God was never absent from the Holy Trinity. The Son of God, as God, is not affected by time and space. As God, He is everywhere. Therefore, while being on earth, He was at the same time up in Heaven, together with the Father and the Holy Spirit.

The question that arises here is: 'Who then ascended up into heaven, since He was there up in Heaven all the time? '

We mentioned above several times that all of the events of Jesus' life, all of His life down here on earth, refers to us; it is absolutely associated with us. His cross is actually our cross, His Resurrection is our resurrection and now His Ascension up into Heaven is actually our ascension up into Heaven. There was no need for Him to ascend up into Heaven because He was always there together with His Father and the Holy Spirit. The Holy Oblation says that very clearly: 'You brought us out of non-existence into being, and when we had fallen you raised us up again, and left nothing undone until you had brought us up to heaven and had granted us your Kingdom that is to come'.

There is a hymn for the Ascension of Christ up into Heaven. The hymn goes: 'The captains of the angels, realizing, O Saviour, the strange quality of the ascension, were asking each other: What is this sight? Yes, it is man seen in his form; yet, as God, beyond heavens, with a body He is ascending'. Here the angels, in a way, are depicted as not being informed about the Ascension. All of a sudden, they see a Man ascending and approaching them. In a way, they wonder what this Man is doing. Man is supposed to belong to a much lower level than them. Therefore, they wonder what Man is doing reaching up towards them. When Man (in the person of the ascending Jesus) is up there with them, their astonishment is even greater. When Man (in the person of the ascending Jesus), continues ascending even above them, their astonishment grows even more. However, when they see Man sitting at the right hand of the Father, they are really astounded with their mouth agape. How could Man be there?

In conclusion, we might say that, ultimately, Jesus' Ascension up into Heaven is not really so much the ascension of the Son of God, but of Man. In other words, the dispensation or Oikonomia has this end: Man's sitting at the right hand of the Father, which ultimately means the deification of Man.

and is seated at the right hand of the Father.

We all know that to place someone at your right hand is an honorific gesture. This seems to have always been the case; certainly at the time of the writing of the Scriptures and of the Creed.

The meaning of the phrase 'at the right hand' is not so much literal as it is essential. In other words, it means that there is no higher position. In the person of Jesus, Man reached the highest spiritual position possible. Man is found at the climax of Man's 'History'.

One might wonder: 'Did Jesus retain His human nature? Was His incarnation not a temporary matter? Did He still have it when ascending up into Heaven? Did He have it when He sat at the right hand of His Father? And finally, does He still have it?' The answer to the above query is that Jesus did not take up human nature in order to get rid of it at some later stage. His incarnation is eternal or even better everlasting. That, of course, shows what great importance Man has in creation. The Creed depicts Man as having a much greater position than the angels. Of course, the angels are the second light from the first light which is God and Man is the third light. However, Man's excellence in the creation lies in Man's uniqueness, being Spirit and Matter at the same time. It seems that in His wisdom God created Man to be eventually superior not only to the rest of the material creation but to the spiritual world as well. Perhaps that is one of the reasons that Satan, the previous archangel of light, the highest of all the spiritual world, became so envious of the creation of Man and tried to take Man away from Man's creator, God, and bring Man to his kingdom of death, which is worse than non-existence.

Article 7

He is coming again in glory to judge the living and the dead and His Kingdom will have no end.

†

He is coming again

The Creed refers to His Second Coming or Advent. The Creed here reassures us that Christ did not just ascend up into Heaven and forgot about us. His promise is to come again. The first time, he came to give Man the opportunity to grasp the salvation that He offers us. He did not come in order to judge us. We shall see below, when we shall deal with Article 11, that this expectation of His Second Advent is predominant in the life of the Christians, especially of the first Church. We can see that particularly in the Acts of the Apostles. We can also see it in the writings of the first Fathers. St. Paul considers himself among those who will be living at the time of Jesus' Second Coming (I Thess. 4.15). It is true that this expectation gives a special essence to the life of the Christians. Even today, if we knew the real 'dimension' of time, we would feel the same way. The enthusiastic element that existed among the first Christians would predominate even today (2,000 years later) and always, if we knew the real essence of time. Time is extended by God just for those who have not yet grasped the opportunity that is offered through Christ to be united with God, the true Life, so that they might be able to do so. His Second Coming will happen in time for those who will still be in this world of space and time. However, in eternity, His Second Coming is happening in no time and in no space. In the Kingdom of God, there is no time and no space. The Kingdom of God is not spatio-temporal. In eternity, existence should be comprehended not in terms of space and time but in terms of states or conditions of being, where there is no movement. This fact, which is inconceivable for us who live in space and time, does not mean that eternity is, in any way, inferior to this world of space and time; on the contrary, it is superior. Space and time mean change and change means wear and wear, ultimately, means death. In eternity, there is no change and therefore no wear and consequently no death. Beings evolve and exist in conditions that the Fathers of our Church call **εστώτα** *(estota)*, a noun, in plural only, which means conditions where there is no movement. One might think that the absence of movement is a negative condition. As living in space and time, this might be true for our own conditions. Yet, even for us, movement means change and change means wear and wear finally means death. Therefore, movement is actually the first reason behind all bad things, death being the worst. The question for us is 'how could there be life without movement?' We forget that the Real Life, which is God Himself, has no movement. If God were moving, then He would change and that would mean wear for Him and eventually death. However, this is impossible. How could He, who is Life Itself, die? However, since there is no movement in God, that means that the absence of movement is an ideal condition. That is what eternity is, among other things: no movement.

From what was mentioned above, we gather that the second coming of Christ will happen *in time* **only** *for those who will be here in this world*. However, for those who will have departed from this world and entered eternity, His Second Coming happens in eternity and not in time. That is why St. Paul says: 'and the dead in Christ will rise **first**. **Then** we who are alive and remain shall be caught up together with them in the clouds to meet the Lord in the air. And thus we shall always be with the Lord' (I Thess. 4.16-17). The word **then**, referring to the 'living', strengthens this idea of the resurrection happening for the 'dead' '**before**' it happens for the 'living'. The reason for these words, **first** and **then,** being used by St. Paul, is the one we have already explained: the resurrection for the 'dead' happens in eternity and therefore not in time.

in glory

His first coming was in humility. His departure, too, from this life was in extreme humility. He was born in a cave, which was being used as a stable. He was born among animals in dirt and stench, as this world He was born in actually was and still is. He departed in the greatest pain and humiliation on the Cross, between two robbers and killers. His second coming is **in glory**. The glory of God has no resemblance to the glory that we know of. People who are accustomed to other kinds of glories, human glories, are not going to be impressed. People, unfortunately, even some 'Christians' among them, await for a glorious Second Advent of His that will be glamorous and clamorous as the glory of this world always is: with a lot of noise, a lot of colours, a lot of brilliant features. They await for something like the welcoming of the new millennium or even greater.

Most people forget that 'the glory of men contains a lot of dangers, whereas that of God gives security and safety' (PG 54,663-664), as St. John Chrysostom says. As far as human glory is concerned, St. John Chrysostom advises us: 'for the present, let us live unnoticed' (PG 57,275-276). 'Human glory renders us into slaves for a myriad of despots or lords who demand various things. If you want to be in love with glory, be in love with the eternal one' (PG 59,243). And St. John Chrysostom goes on: 'Then will I become brilliant and will I enjoy a greater glory, when I ignore glory' (PG 60,120), 'we should ignore glory. We should better be objects of mockery rather than of credit' (PG 60,364-365), 'Those who have glorified God, they will much more be glorified. Glory is the sorrow for Christ. The more we are humiliated, the more we become brilliant' (PG 62,481).

'When something is **not** done for the glory of God, even if it is a spiritual act, it may harm us to the utmost' (PG 48,962). 'Whatever we do, we do everything for the glory of God' (PG 48,962).

Concerning the future glory, St. John Chrysostom says: 'That is why our Lord Jesus Christ came, so that not only do we see the present glory but the future one as well' (PG 59,85). 'The harm that those who will be deprived of that glory will suffer is immeasurable. Let us then struggle so that we may be worthy of enjoying that one' (PG 59,86). 'Whatever we suffer in this life is nothing in value in comparison to the glory that is going to be revealed' (PG 60,529). 'The present glory is nothing and it is unstable too. That one (the heavenly glory) is stable and it will have no end. Because that glory is from within' (PG 62,512). 'There is no more worthy thing than that glory' (PG 62,512-513). 'The real glory exists only in Heaven' (PG 62,621-24).

The honourary professor of the Theological school of the University of Athens Andreas Theodorou, in his book entitled *'The Theology of the Light of Glory"* (in Greek), in his prologue, says: 'For someone to speak about God (Theology-theologian) is a difficult thing. Man's language is very poor and weak in Man's endeavour to touch his transcendental object: the infinite and 'uncontainable' God... The chasm that separates the two natures (divine and human)

The Creed

is abysmal and unbridgeable. No created nature, no power, which is outside God, can ever contain the transcendental essence of God, neither in the present nor in the future age. Only the hypostases of the Holy Trinity, the Father, the Son and the Holy Spirit, can comprehend the essence of God. Nobody else' (p.7). Therefore, nobody can comprehend His glory either. The glory that God is lies beyond any perception. We can perceive His glory up to a certain extent: with the perception with which we are endowed by Him. The reason for that is not that He does not want us to perceive the wholeness of His glory; it is because of the natural supreme difference that exists between the created and uncreated nature. This does not mean that we are deprived by our creator. It is because of the natural difference between the two natures. However, the degree in which we can perceive His glory is not to be scorned. On the contrary, it is the greatest bliss that Man can ever have. What is usually called, the uncreated Light, is actually God's Glory. What God, let us say, may be 'proud' of, beyond His essence, is this Light of His. It is His glory. There is no greater glory than that. It can be perceived only by those who are able; only people who have acquired, to the degree that Man can, the attributes of God. The most important of all these qualities, even beyond true justice, divine love and freedom, is absolute simplicity. It is the quality that contains many other qualities, the greatest of which is humility. How could one who is not absolutely simple see Simplicity in its absolute grandeur? It is not without significance that Jesus' first words on the Mount were: 'Blessed are the poor in spirit, for theirs is the Kingdom of Heaven' (Matt. 5.3). Who are these *poor in spirit*? Even 'Christians' pour scorn on those who are *poor in spirit*. They are considered stupid, to say the least. Yes, *the poor in spirit* are really stupid or even crazy for this world. Those who are *poor in spirit* are never considered successful in this life. Only those who acquire a lot of wealth or glory or great positions are considered successful in this life. However, Jesus Himself tells us: 'Do not lay up for yourselves treasures on earth, where moth and rust destroy and where thieves break in and steal' (Matt. 6.19). Jesus advises us: 'But lay up for yourselves treasures in heaven, where neither moth nor rust destroys, and where thieves do not break in and steal' (Matt. 6.20). Why then should we be careful about where our treasures are? Jesus tells us that as well: 'For where your treasure is, there will your heart be also' (Matt. 6.21).

In the same way, the glory, in which Jesus will come again, is of a similar nature. It is similar to the Light that God is. This Light that God is is not similar to the light that we know of. The light that we know does not help us to understand that Light. On the contrary, it makes it more difficult for us to be able to see the Real Light. This fact is one of the good things that the blind have. The blind will find it easier to see the True Light for exactly this reason: that they have never seen this light. The Light that God is cannot be seen with the eyes that we have and in the same process as that of sight. The light we see is an object, a stimulus, that the eyes (the receptors) catch and bring to the appropriate part of the brain, where it is analyzed and 'translated' into vision. We can understand that God cannot be an object of sight or a stimulus for our eyes. The same applies to His Light. It cannot be perceived through the eyes. It is perceived through another kind of vision much higher than the one we are aware of. If we do not develop the higher senses, we shall not be able to hear the sounds of eternity; we shall not be able to see the sights of eternity; we shall not be able to smell, taste, touch and feel in general the things of the eternity.

In order to 'see' the uncreated Light of God, one must reach the level of divine darkness, which actually means total ignorance (Vladimir Lossky, *The Mystical Theology of the Eastern Church*, James Clarke & Co. Ltd, London, p. 25). This is what is meant by the psalm: 'He made darkness His secret place; His canopy around Him was dark waters and thick clouds of the skies' (Psalm 18.11). We have to accept our incapacity to reach the true knowledge of God. We must actually be poor in spirit, to be able to proceed and reach the true knowledge and even 'see' the uncreated Light of God. This is the supreme bliss that we may ever be able to have in this life. This bliss will be at its highest when Jesus comes again in all of His glory.

to judge the living and the dead

to judge

His first Coming was not to judge; it was to save Man, the sinner. Man could not justify himself by himself. Sin could only be erased by God. Therefore, the Father sent His Son to save Man from sin and the state of death which was of Satan, to whom Man was a mere slave. As Man could not save himself, Man could not justify himself in any way. That is why the Son of God took on human nature: in order to save Man.

This was the purpose of His first coming. The purpose of His Second Coming is to judge. God is, among other things, Justice, real Justice. Therefore, His Second Coming is to fulfill this attribute of His. He cannot be unjust. He cannot give the same things to those who struggled greatly for His glory and suffered and reached the point of sacrificing themselves for His name, as He will give to those who struggled much less and never suffered and never sacrificed anything. He cannot treat in the same way those who were on the opposite 'front' of the spiritual battle for the victory of the good and for the justification and glorification of the Lamb. His Justice cannot accept those who were ruthless and never showed any sign of love to those who were in any kind of need. Divine Justice demands love on the part of Man; it demands freedom. Those who deprive their fellow men of their freedom will have no place in His Kingdom. Those who were not simple cannot be in company with the One who is Simplicity Itself.

Divine Justice is fairness in its absolute form. God is absolutely fair. That does not mean that He reaches the extreme. The Latins used to say: 'summum ius, summa iniuria', which means 'extreme justice, extreme injustice', meaning that when the search for justice goes beyond certain limits, then this justice becomes injustice. Of course, God never goes to the extremes in His Justice. On the contrary, He shows more leniency than Man ever does. He is ready to forgive anyone who repents or regrets for his previous unjust life. That is why He first came down to earth. However, that does not mean that He will forgive those who have never taken the opportunity to change their lives; those who persisted in leading a life away from Him in sheer injustice, absence of love and freedom and where there was not a sign of modesty and humility. He cannot be unfair to those who struggled and suffered and sacrificed everything, even their lives, for His glory and in order that justice, love and freedom prevail in the world.

The parable about His Second Coming is very illuminating. He will not call to His right side all those who were **supposed** to be His: bishops and the rest of the clergy, theologians, church-goers and the like. He will call to His Kingdom all those who were benevolent to their fellow men. There is no other category that is mentioned here for those who are destined to inherit the Kingdom of God. Bishops and the rest of the clergy, theologians and church-goers might be among those who will inherit the Kingdom of God. They are not excluded from It, of course. However, they are not going to inherit It because they were what they were. On the contrary, they will find it more difficult to enter the Kingdom of God. Because they are supposed to have been better examples of love towards their fellow men than the others. They know better and they are liable to be judged more severely than the rest. However, we should always have in mind that the only criterion for inheriting the Kingdom of God is love, practical love, towards our fellow men. Love towards our fellow men is love towards God Himself. Jesus says that very clearly: 'Assuredly, I say to you, inasmuch as you did *it* to one of the least of these My brethren, you did *it* to Me' (Matt. 25.40).

the living

Who are these? Our Church Fathers knew very well who the living really are. The living are actually those who are united with Life Itself; no matter if they live here on earth or in eternity. Dead are those who are not united with Life Itself either here or in eternity. However, they were obliged to accept the general notions of those times. It is in fact the idea that most people have today more than ever. In fact, how many people today, even 'Christians', believe that those who depart from this life really live in eternity? Very few. And those who do, believe that it is not the whole of those who depart that continue to live (soul and body), but only a part of them (their soul). They even believe that their soul is found in a state of expectancy for the resurrection of the dead which will happen in the future. They forget that once we depart from this world of space and time, we are found in eternity where there is no space and no time. And since there is no time, the period of expectancy has no meaning at all. The Second Coming of Christ will be in time for those who will be living in this universe of space and time. For those who have departed and therefore do not belong to space and time but to eternity, the resurrection takes place in eternity, where there is no space and time.

and the dead

Who are these? Are they the ones who have departed from this life of space and time? What do we mean by the word *dead*? Do we mean that they really do not live? We know that this is absolutely wrong. Because if that was the case, then St. Paul and all the apostles and all the saints are dead, that is: they do not live. However, we know that they live; and they live, one could say, more than we do. They live more because they are in eternity and eternity is closer to the everlasting God. They are immensely closer to the Real Life than we are. They have real life in them.

The early Church established the word *cemetery* for the place that the departed are placed. *Cemetery* comes from the Greek word **κοιμητήριο** *(koimeterio)*, which means 'a place of sleep'. The word comes from the Greek verb **κοιμούμαι** *(koimoume)*, which means *I sleep*. And those who have departed are called **κεκοιμημένοι** *(kekoimeménoi)* by the Church. This means 'the ones who are asleep'. This idea of *kekoimeménoi* is closer to reality rather than the word *dead*. Of course, it does not mean that those who have departed are found in some kind of sleep. On the contrary, they live a life that is far from anything resembling sleep. The idea of sleep suits the idea of time related to what happens in eternity. During sleep, the function of the sense of time ceases to exist. Therefore, time does not exist for the one who is sleeping. That is what is happening with the departed. Since they belong to eternity, where there is no time, time ceases to exist for them. And when the resurrection takes place in time for the 'living' and in eternity for the 'dead', then it is the 'living' that will enter eternity and therefore the ceasing of time, and not vice versa.

and His Kingdom will have no end

and

The word *and* means an addition to the things that were said above. In this case, though, the meaning of *and* is even stronger. The end of our present life, even the end of this world as a whole does not mean the end of existence. Our personal existence does not end at the moment of our biological death. It continues into eternity. This physical world will be succeeded by another which is not merely superior but incomparable to this one. It is the one that follows the word *and*.

His Kingdom

The Kingdom of God. It is also called the Kingdom of Heaven. St. Matthew never uses the former. He always uses the latter: *the Kingdom of Heaven*. He does that because he wants to continue the

The Creed

Jewish custom of not mentioning the name of God. The name of God is too sacred to come to people's lips. This is according to the third commandment which says: 'You shall not take the name of the Lord your God in vain; for the Lord will not hold him guiltless that takes His name in vain' (Ex. 20.7).

The word *kingdom* does not sound so appropriate these days. Royal dynasties, with very few exceptions (as is the case of the king or queen of England), have failed. There are almost no kings nowadays. Where there still are, they do not function in any other way but as mere decorative institutions. Authority, which is based on hereditary custom, is no longer accepted. The majority of the kings of the past failed to capture the love of their subordinates because they used their authority in an arbitrary and ruthless manner. The idea of democracy has captured the favour of everybody. The idea that people themselves should elect their governors has won over the whole world. It was first established in ancient Athens and it has spread to the whole world especially recently. It is natural that the term *kingdom* does not sound pleasant in the ears of modern Man.

Why do we not change the word? There are many reasons for it. One of them is that we should always go back to the times that something was written. In those days, there was no other kind of rule than that of monarchy. The usual kind of ruler was either a king or an emperor. An empire was actually a very big kingdom. Another reason is what lies behind the word *kingdom*. It meant power, absolute power. Of course, there is no comparison between the power of a ruler and the power of God. The difference does not merely lie in the greatness of power, but in the kind of power. Naturally, there is no comparison as far as greatness is concerned between the two. Earthly kingdoms are nothing in greatness in comparison with the Heavenly Kingdom. Earthly kingdoms are transient, too, whereas the Kingdom of God is permanent; it has no end, as the Creed says. The Heavenly Kingdom has the eternal God as Its Head. An earthly kingdom has a king, who is a mortal human being, no different from the others, as its head.

There is also an immense difference between the two as far as the exercise of their power is concerned. Jesus Himself told His disciples: 'You know that the rulers of the Gentiles lord it over them, and those who are great exercise authority over them. Yet it shall not be so among you; but whoever desires to become great among you, let him be your servant. And whoever desires to be first among you, let him be your slave – just as the Son of Man did not come to be served, but to serve, and to give His life a ransom for many' (Matt. 20.25-28). There is no need to explain. Jesus is absolutely clear.

The reality of the Kingdom of God must be as clear as possible in our minds. Therefore, it is imperative to know more about it. First of all, we must not confuse it with the notion of *paradise*. Unfortunately, most people confuse the Kingdom of God with paradise. When we say paradise, our mind usually goes to the idea of an extremely beautiful garden full of fruit trees of all kinds. It is true that the Old Testament mentions *paradise*. However, even that paradise cannot be a garden of fruit trees. This can be gathered from the fact that the story of the Old Testament tells us about two trees that existed in the middle of paradise or the garden of Eden: the tree of life and the tree of the knowledge of good and evil. We know very well that such trees do not exist. The reason is that there have never been such trees. The word 'tree' here means something completely different from that of the concept of a tree. We are not going to go into the question of what these trees really represent, as that would take a very long and involved exposition. In a few words, though: the tree of life is Jesus Himself and His Cross which saves us and gives us real Life. The tree of the knowledge of good and evil is a reality. This reality was destined for Man to know in the process of his deification. According to St. Gregory of Nanzianzus, the Theologian, Man would not only be allowed, at some point in his process towards deification, to 'taste' the 'fruit' of this 'tree' but it would be imperative for him to do so. Man's fall is due not to the fact that he tried it, but because, in addition to his disobedience to God, he was still too immature to 'taste' it. This tells us that paradise was not really a garden; even though it is also called the *Garden of Eden*. Paradise must be rather the Kingdom of God or of Heaven. That is why sometimes the Kingdom of God is referred to as paradise. Therefore, when we come across the word *paradise*, we must right away think of the Kingdom of God and not of a garden of fruit trees.

Jesus gave us, through His disciples, a prayer, which we recite most often. The prayer, among other things, says: '..thy Kingdom come, thy will be done on earth as in heaven'. In this prayer we beg that His Kingdom will come. This means that we are seeking It. We are looking forward to It. It means that we are struggling for a world where the will of God is observed everywhere and by everybody.

The most revealing description of the Kingdom of God is provided by our Lord Jesus Christ. After the miracle with the cleansing of the ten lepers, the Pharisees asked Him about the time that the Kingdom of God would come. Jesus answered: 'The kingdom of God does not come with observation, nor will they say, 'See here!' or, 'See there!' For indeed, the kingdom of God is within you' (Luke 17. 20-21). We learn here, from the mouth of Jesus Himself, that the Kingdom of God is not something that you can observe like everything else. This is so with everything which is spiritual. Eternity is a reality; angels as well; and God Himself. However, it is a reality of a different kind. We are accustomed to this material world of ours and it is extremely difficult, if not impossible, for us to comprehend spiritual things. An example from ourselves: we are flesh and spirit. We can see our body; we cannot see our souls. Everybody agrees that we have an inner world. Where is that? Man has thought, through the ages, of various places inside his body where the seat of this inner world might be. Some thought the heart; some the spleen; some the kidneys and so on. There have been so many operations performed on all of these internal organs. No doctor has ever reported any sign whatsoever of an inner world. So, where is this inner world? The answer is: 'nowhere!' That does not mean that the inner world does

The Creed

not exist. God is nowhere, from the point of view that He is not in any space. He could not be. If He were in some space, that would mean that He would be confined in it. We know that God is infinite and unconfined. We might say that the same, at a much lower level, of course, happens with spiritual beings or conditions. Let us return to the inner world. The inner world is of a spiritual nature. As such it is not contained within a certain space. It is real; it is a fact but not the way our body is. Our body, as a material object, occupies a specified space every time. Our inner world is absolutely linked with it but not in the physical fashion that we know of. It is 'connected' with our body in a metaphysical manner. Of course, you cannot have your body 'here' and your inner world 'there'. Anyway, the ideas of here and there do not apply in the case of spiritual matters. When Jesus says that the Kingdom of God cannot be observed here or there, He means, first, that the Kingdom of God cannot be perceived by our natural senses and secondly that It cannot be found in space but within us. When He says inside us, He does not mean in the inside part of our body but in our inner world. Our inner world is not found in space even though our inner world is closely linked with our body. Therefore, we can draw the conclusion that the Kingdom of God, as well as Hades, is found in us. It is strange how we can be found in the Kingdom of God or in Hades and at the same time have the same in us. These mysteries will be revealed to us as soon as we enter eternity. At present, we cannot comprehend the 'dimensions' of eternity. Jesus said to His disciples: '...it has been given to you to know the mysteries of the kingdom of heaven, but to them it has not been given' (Matt. 13.11). Why is it given to His disciples and not to some others? Who are 'them'? The answer to the above questions is His parable of the sower. The reason why the mysteries are granted to some and not to others is the 'soil' in which the 'seed' of the logos is 'sown'. The key to the whole subject lies in repentance. The Greek word for repentance is **μετάνοια** *(metanoia)*. It is coined from the words **μετά** *(meta)* and **νους** *(nous)*. The first does not mean the usual *after* but it is related to the concept of **μεταβολή** *(metabole)*, which means change. **Νους** *(nous)* usually means mind or brain. Here it means mentality or manner of thinking and acting or the philosophy of life that one has. If we want to be with God, we are supposed to be like God. Among other things, God is just; therefore, we must be just ourselves. God is love; therefore, we must have love towards our fellow men and to Him. God is freedom; therefore, we must keep our freedom and not enslave it to our weaknesses and our passions and we must not deprive our fellow-men of their freedom either; God is Simplicity; therefore, we must be simple and humble and poor in spirit. No matter how strange this may sound, the latter is the hardest of all. However, it is the most important as well. In English simplicity is very much linked with stupidity. It is true that, for human standards simplicity is stupidity. However, simplicity is the supreme attribute of God. We either accept that or we must forget about closeness to God. We must forget about having any revelations of the mysteries of God; in this case the mysteries of His Kingdom.

will have no end ('of His Kingdom there will be no end' Luke. 1.33)

It goes without saying that the Kingdom of God will have no end. God has no end and so His Kingdom has no end either. It has no end because it is not merely eternal but everlasting. The difference between eternal and everlasting is that eternity is the cessation of time; 'everlastingness' is beyond even that. Everlastingness has no relation to time whatsoever, even a negative one. This fact is assured by St. Luke, when he says: 'and of His kingdom there will be no end' (Luke 1.33). Of course, Luke is talking about an earthly kingdom that Jesus was supposed to establish. Of course, it is eventually proved that His Kingdom has no relation with earthly kingdoms, as we mentioned above. This was actually a great disillusionment for the people who followed Him, even for His disciples. Some have said that Judas was so disillusioned by the words of Jesus that He was about to be arrested and put to death, that He decided to betray Him. Others believe that he intentionally betrayed Jesus in order to force Him to proceed to His rebellion against the Romans as soon as possible and then establish his own kingdom. Jesus is more than clear when He says to Pontius Pilate: 'MY KINGDOM IS NOT OF THIS WORLD: If my Kingdom were of this world, then would my servants fight, that I should not be delivered to the Jews: but now MY KINGDOM IS NOT OF THIS WORLD' (John 18. 36).

His disciples believed approximately the same things about Him as Judas did. Even his close disciples believed that He would establish His own kingdom. And they had ambitions about their place in that kingdom. Up to the last minute they had such dreams about Jesus. It was after the illumination that came from the Holy Spirit on the Pentecost that their minds were illuminated as to who really Jesus was and what the purpose of His first coming was.

We all know from experience that earthly kingdoms are transient. They are established, they grow, they come to their climax and then they come to know their fall and extinction. However, the Kingdom of God has no end. God's Kingdom had no beginning. We know from Philosophy that everything that has a beginning has an end as well. And anything that has no beginning has no end either. The latter is only God or anything related to Him. Since His Kingdom has no beginning it has no end either.

The Kingdom of God will not begin with the Second Coming of Christ. The Kingdom of God already exists. As we mentioned above, it has no beginning. It existed before all ages. It is everlasting like God. And as it existed everlastingly, it will continue existing likewise.

Article 8

And in the Holy Spirit, the Lord, the Giver of Life, who proceeds from the Father, who together with Father and Son is worshipped and together glorified; who spoke through the prophets.

✝

And in the Holy Spirit

Spirit. The word that is used in Greek, the language in which the Creed was originally written, is *πνεῦμα (pneuma)*. This word comes from the verb *πνέω (pneo)*, which means *I blow* like a wind does. Therefore, *πνεῦμα* actually means something like *a gust of wind*.

It is easy to see that the word does not tell us exactly what the *Spirit* is. Human language is absolutely incapable of describing or expressing things that are not in the field of Man's perception, imagination or deduction. The *Spirit* is wholly outside Man's conception, comprehension, description and expression. In general, we might say that the word *spirit* conveys the opposite notion to the word *matter*. The latter is found in space and time. Conversely, the *spirit* 'functions' outside space and time. It is not found at any specific space, and cannot be measured with time. Of course, in this world, the *spirit* functions and is in connection with matter but it is not infused into it. For instance, the brain is found in a particular space (the skull), and functions there but its 'product' is not confined there. That is why the function of the synapses in the brain is vague and undefined; especially its outcome as found in the spiritual field.

In the Creed we do not just say *Spirit*; we say *Holy Spirit*. What does *Holy* mean, though? God alone is Holy. Therefore, the Spirit we believe in is God. The word *holy* means *perfect to the highest degree from all aspects*.

We might say that the Holy Spirit is neither *holy* nor *spirit*. This is contradictory to what has already been said. What we mean by that is that the words *spirit* and *holy* are infinitely weak in defining or expressing the Holy Spirit. This does not mean that It is a vague notion; it means that God (and, therefore, the Holy Spirit) is indefinable, unutterable and incomprehensible.

Many people wonder whether there is such a thing as the *Holy Spirit*. In other words: Is It real? Some people believe that reality is only that which we can perceive. In the twentieth century, however, modern physicists discovered that even the physical world is not to be taken for granted. Heisenberg's principle of uncertainty claims that the world, which science examines and studies, is not at all as concrete as scientists used to think it was. Furthermore, the quantum theory and quantum mechanics have shaken the foundations of classical Newtonian Physics. The reality of the material world that people of the past (especially the materialists) knew, is no longer as firm and solid as it used to be. Science, which is based on observation, analysis, experimentation and mathematics, can no longer assert that it is based on any certainty as in what reality really is. How can we then assert that we are being so specific when we are dealing with metaphysical matters such as this one?

The Fathers of our Church introduced another kind of theology in addition to the *cataphatic (positive)* one. The former is called *apophatic* theology. *Cataphatic* theology tells us what God **is**. *Apophatic* theology tells us what God **is not.** The latter is closer to the truth. It is not easy to say what God is. On the contrary, it is impossible. That is why we said above that the Holy Spirit is neither holy nor spirit. What *apophatic* theology means is that it is impossible to have the true concept of *holy* or *spirit* in our mind. It would be a great deception to say that we have the right concept of *spirit* or *holy* in our mind. We might as well say that the general concept of *spirit* is close to the concept of immaterial. It exists but it is immaterial. Of course, this can never be conceived by those for whom the concept of reality is only the one that can be perceived and nothing else. For them, the concept of *spirit* does not belong to the 'field' of reality. For them, the *spirit* belongs to the realm of fantasy.

The Holy Spirit is the model of every spiritual *hypostasis*. Since the Father is not matter, what proceeds from Him is Spirit. It is the Person without whom neither the spiritual nor the material world, nor Man would be granted existence. The Holy Spirit is the Person of the Holy Trinity which is true Light. From this Light, the spiritual world is detached. That is why the angels are a 'flow' of the first Light which is God. We might as well say that angels are not the 'flow' of the Father or of the Son but of the Holy Spirit. That is why they are called spiritual world. This does not mean that the Holy Spirit is of a lower standard than the other two Persons of the Holy Trinity. On the contrary, we might risk saying, It is the most 'refined' of the Three. When God 'decided' to create the worlds (the spiritual and the material), He decided to create them from His most 'refined' Person, which was sent forth or proceeded from the 'depths' of the Father. In this way, the Father, with His Will, creates the worlds through His Son in the Spirit of His infinite love and benevolence.

Let us see what the Acts of the Apostles tell us about it: 'When the Day of Pentecost had fully come, they were all with one accord in one place. And suddenly there came **a sound from heaven, as of a rushing mighty wind**, and it **filled the whole house** where they were sitting. Then there appeared to them **divided tongues, as of fire**, and *one* sat upon each of them. And they were all **filled with the Holy Spirit**, and began to speak with other tongues, as the Spirit gave them utterance' (Acts 2.1-4).

The Creed

The action of the Holy Spirit here is described as a rushing mighty wind. At the baptism of Jesus It was described as resembling a dove. Here it is described as cloven tongues like as of fire. Clearly, there is a difference between a dove and a tongue of fire. And there is a great difference between them and a gust of mighty wind. What is the Holy Spirit, then? It could not be all of them. They do not even resemble each other. A dove and tongues of fire are far from similar. And a gust of wind can be felt and heard but not seen. There must be some explanation.

The Holy Spirit can be whatever it wishes to be. It could be anything and it is nothing of these things or anything that it could be. Can the Holy Spirit be a dove? God forbid! And It cannot be tongues of fire or a gust of wind either. It would be a blasphemy to say that It is any of those things or any thing. And it is actually unorthodox to depict any of those as being the Holy Spirit. Especially when the Holy Trinity is depicted as the Father being like an old man and the Holy Spirit as being a dove. The only Person that can be depicted is Jesus and that is so because the Son of God took on human nature. It is very important to note that the Bible uses the word *like* or *as* or both.

The Holy Spirit is also called the Paraclete. The word comes from the Greek word **Παράκλητος** *(Paracletos)* and the Greek verb that it comes from is **παρακαλώ** *(parakalo)*, which, among other things, means *I call for help* or *I make a petition*. It also means *I console* or *I give comfort or relief* or even *I claim or I ask somebody to act as my defender*. Therefore, *Paraclete* might be some kind of *Defender* *or* Comforter. Jesus Himself speaks about this Comforter when He says to His disciples: 'And I will pray the Father, and He will give you another Helper, that He may abide with you for ever - the Spirit of Truth, whom the world cannot receive, because it neither sees Him, nor knows Him; but you know Him, for He dwells with you and will be in you' (John 14.16-17).

We can see here that the Holy Spirit remains unknown to those who are not ready to know It. Those who are ready to know It, they know It not like one knows something through the senses but from spiritual experience. The Holy Spirit is among those who accept the work of the dispensation of Jesus, as His disciples do. The Holy Spirit is also in them. He resides in the depths of their inner world. In other words, by saying this, Jesus means that the Holy Spirit is concealed from the eyes of most people. At the same time, the Holy Spirit is evident to the chosen ones. The latter are those who are the eternal disciples of Christ: those who accept Him in their lives which they devote to Him in all humility.

We shall be able to know more about the Holy Spirit with what follows in the Creed.

the Lord

Firstly, what is the meaning of the word? It usually refers to God, especially when it is written with capital L. In Greek the word is **Κύριος** (*Kyrios*) (a word that is used in *Kyrie eleison!* = *Lord have* *mercy!*). It is possible that it comes from the Greek word *κύρος* (*kyros*), which means *prestige*, which we come across in Sanskrit as *sura*, which means *powerful*. The idea of Lordship means absolute ownership or power and authority. This is not far from the meaning of the Hebrew word *Adon,* or even better its plural *Adonai*. This is used by the Jews, for reverence, instead of *Jehovah*, which means God. *Adon* means *the one who has absolute control, the master,* or even *the king.*

This title is often used for people. In English, Lords are those who are members of the House of Lords. In Greek, even today, all men (male) are called *κύριος* (kyrios), naturally with a small *κ – k*, *equivalent to the English word Mister.* The word is also used by slaves when addressing or referring to their master. The reason is that they feel and know that they belong to him. Another connotation of the word is that *the lord,* whoever he may be, is independent from anybody else. He does not belong to anybody else. He can stand by himself. In religious terminology, when we are using the word Lord, we refer to God exclusively.

The Holy Spirit is the Lord. Now, one might be mystified. 'Well, who is the Lord?' one might ask. 'Is it the Father or the Son or the Holy Spirit?' The answer to this question is of vital importance. God is the Lord. However, who is God? We say at the beginning of the Creed: 'I believe in one God'. Therefore, we establish that God is one and, of course, He is the Lord. Again, at the beginning of the Creed, we say: 'I believe in one God, Father almighty.' Therefore, we now know that the Lord is the Father. However, a little further down, we say: 'And in one **Lord**, Jesus Christ, the only-begotten Son of God". And then, we say: 'And in the Holy Spirit, the Lord.' How can three Persons be the Lord? It is a very logical question. Now, let us see certain cases from the Bible. At some point, Jesus addresses His Father and says: 'I thank You, Father, Lord of heaven and earth' (Luke 10.21). Therefore, here we can hear Jesus Himself call His Father *Lord*. One might say that since His Father is the Lord, He Himself (that is: Jesus) cannot be the Lord as well. Things are not as plain as we think in human terms, when we refer to divine matters. Jesus, the Son of the Father, acknowledges the Fatherhood of His Father. He would not be His Father if there were not this relation between Them. Even though the Son 'knows' very well that He Himself is the maker of everything, He also 'knows' that the cause of everything is His Father. Everything is due to His Father's will. Even with human relations, the father assigns his son to do something. First of all, the son knows that if it were not for his father, He would not exist. Then his father gives him the tools to make certain things. His father tells him how to make them. It was his father's decision to make what the son makes. If his father did not wish it, then the things would not have been made.

Above, we dealt with the Holy Spirit. In the Creed, we say: 'And in the Holy Spirit'. Here, the phrase 'I believe' is implied. Therefore, actually it is as if we were saying: 'I believe also in the Holy Spirit'. Therefore, our belief is threefold: in the Father, the Son and the Holy

Spirit. This does not mean that we believe in three gods. Anyway, we are very clear about that from the beginning. We say: 'I believe in ONE God'. The fact that we believe in the Father, the Son and the Holy Spirit means that, yes, 'the' God I believe in is ONE but He is not ONE person, as it happens e.g. in Islam, but He is three Persons or Hypostases. This does not make Him inferior to the one-person god but immensely superior and, above everything else, this makes Him the true God. He is superior to the one-person god, because the latter:

a) does not communicate with His (actually non-existing) equal(s); anyone who is con-substantial with Him, as there is no other person than Him. If there were such a god, He would, first of all, feel lonely. Our God, the true God, does not feel lonely. Every and each one of the Three Persons has two others to communicate with.

b) cannot be Love Itself. How can he be Love when there is/are no other person(s) like Him to love? Love cannot be a theoretical matter. Love must be practised in order to really exist. Again, if this one-person god loves Himself, this means that He is the most egotistical, selfish and ego-centric being that one could think of.

Our God is Love because Love is exchanged between the three Persons. Without this Love, God would not be One. The oneness of God is ensured by the Love that unites the three of them into an absolute unity. This unity cannot be achieved without this Love that is exchanged by the three Persons in their relation with each other.

c) cannot be Simplicity, which is the basic attribute of God. How could a one-person god be simple, when he has no one of the same substance to show His simplicity to. He cannot be simple to his creation because they are not of the same substance as Him.

However, simplicity makes it possible for God to be united. It is through simplicity that God, even though He is three Persons, is One. How could more than one god be absolutely simple?

However, we have not yet established how not only the Father could be the Lord; that the other two Persons can each one of them be the Lord. The Father does not beget the Son or send forth the Holy Spirit to be inferior to Him. He begets His Son so that He be equal to Him in everything. The same applies with the Holy Spirit. Anyway, the three of Them have the same substance and nature. They are just different Persons or Hypostases. And as far as us Men are concerned, we usually refer to one of the Persons each time. And when we refer to each one of them, we refer to divinity as a whole. We do not, and we should not, have the feeling that we are referring to one third of divinity but to the whole of God. And God is the Lord. Furthermore, each Person is a completely different Person. One cannot be confused with the other. Therefore, each one of them is an individual hypostasis. And as we, men, are considered to be independent and separate from other human beings, the same applies, with greater force, to each and every Person of the Holy Trinity. For all the above reasons, each person is the Lord.

the Giver of Life

Yes, the Holy Spirit is the giver of life; one might add: the creator of life.

In one of the most common prayers of our Church, which is actually addressed to the Holy Spirit, we say: 'Heavenly King, Paraclete, Spirit of Truth, present everywhere, filling all things, Treasury of Blessings and **Giver of Life...**' The Holy Spirit is the one that not only gives life but creates life as well: biological life but true Life as well, which is God Himself. In other words, the Holy Spirit gives us God Himself.

The Holy Spirit is the One who takes care for us to come to know Jesus' word for our salvation and to be united with God Himself, who is the true Life. The Holy Spirit is Life Itself. He is not only the true Life but He is also all those things that accompany divine Life. That is why we say in the above prayer: **Treasury of blessings**. The Holy Spirit does not want to have all these things for Himself only. One might say that He is struggling to transmit or convey all these good things to us. However, this can be done only in freedom. If Man does not want them, then the Holy Spirit cannot give them to us. Why does the Holy Spirit mind our freedom so much? The answer is: because it is He Who gives Man his freedom; how then could He Himself take it away from Man? And how do we know that He is the giver of freedom? Because freedom is one of the most precious blessings that Man has. And, as we said above, all good things are His.

He is the giver of life. We can see the Holy Spirit giving life in the first lines of the Holy Bible: 'And the earth was without form, and void; and darkness was upon the face of the deep. And the **Spirit of God moved upon the face of the waters**' (Gen. 1.2).

Here, we can see the Holy Spirit sitting *'like a hen'* is sitting upon its eggs hatching them; that is: trying to give life to them. The Bible here depicts the Holy Spirit as transferring Its own Life to a creation that was, let us say in a very simple way, 'under construction'. The Bible here is very clear. The Father decides and His Logos (or His Word), that is, His Son goes on and creates the world that His Father wants to be created. And the Holy Spirit starts His work of giving life to the creation of the Son. The Son is depicted as creating the waters: this basic form of matter. And the Holy Spirit sits upon this basic matter and gives it life. And later, when all the world is made, the Holy Spirit undertakes the government of it. Without the Holy Spirit, this world that was created by the Son and given life by the Holy Spirit, would not be able to be governed well, as it is governed, without the work of the Holy Spirit. Therefore, the Holy Spirit is not only the creator of life, but It is also the governor of the creation.

Further on, in Genesis, we read: 'And the Lord God formed man of dust of the ground, and **breathed into his nostrils the breath of life; and man became a living soul'** (Gen. 2.7). Here, we can see another work of God. He breathes into the nostrils of man, who was, up to then, mere dust of the ground. What is this breath of God? We cannot think of God as breathing like us. God is not like man; God does not breathe. He does not have any mouth and lungs to breathe with. What is this breath of life, then? It is nothing else but the Holy Spirit, that enters Man and makes him **a living soul.** In other words, the Holy Spirit makes Man spiritual. From that time onwards, Man is no longer a mere animal. Man is an animal, but an animal that is in the process of being deified. Now, Man is a mixture of the two worlds of the creation: the spiritual and the material. Man is now a part of two worlds: the spiritual and the material. He belongs more to the spiritual, when he freely wants it to be so. And this is all the work of the Holy Spirit, because the Father wishes it. That is one of the reasons that St. Paul considers Man's body to be the temple of the Holy Spirit (I Cor. 3.16-17).

who proceeds from the Father

The proceeding of the Holy Spirit from the Father, as well as other words that are used in relation to our faith are far from capable of rendering the meaning of such realities. The proceeding is inconceivable by our mind. It is a similar energy of the Father to that of the begetting of the Son, yet not the same. We might say that, as the Son is the only-begotten Son, so is the Holy Spirit the 'only-proceeding Spirit'. As the Father does not beget any other Son, so no other Spirit proceeds from Him. The proceeding comes from the substance of the Father Himself. That is why the Holy Spirit is consubstantial with the Father and the Son. As we said above, the Holy Spirit, let us say, is the most 'refined' Person of the divinity. Not only is It not of a lower standard, because It is the Third and therefore the last, but It is the Holy Spirit that 'gives worth' to the divinity. Without It, the divinity would not have been whole; it would lack its most perfect 'part'. Perhaps that is the reason that only the Spirit, of all three Persons, is called Holy. Not that the other two are not Holy. However, the idea of perfection in the divinity is focused on the Holy Spirit.

Its proceeding is from the source of the divinity, that is: the Father. This occurs in an incomprehensible and mystical fashion.

The Roman Catholics added the phrase *Filioque*, which means 'from the Son as well'. They added it centuries after the Third Ecumenical Synod which had decided that nothing should be added to or taken away from the Creed composed during the first and second Ecumenical Synods. This decision was taken with the illumination of the Holy Spirit Itself. With the arbitrary addition of the *Filioque*, not only is the decision of Third Synod violated but the position of the Holy Spirit within the Holy Trinity is distorted as well. It is presented not only as inferior to the other two Persons but also as some kind

The Creed

of servant to them. This is absolutely unacceptable. Furthermore, with the *Filioque*, the truth, as it is given by the spirit of the New Testament, is gone. According to it, we might say that each Person knows Its 'function' within the Holy Trinity: the Father begets the Son and proceeds the Holy Spirit. And the two Persons, the Son and the Holy Spirit, 'obey' the Father. Neither of them has an independent will; they both 'carry out' the will of the Father. Of course, the term 'Father' refers to the Son, whom the Father begets. However, the word Father has been established in reference to the first Person. Actually, the first Person of the Holy Trinity, in relation to the Third Person, is the 'proceeder', and this is so because He does not beget It but proceeds It. However, this is done only by the first Person and not by the Son, as well. The role of the Son is not to cause the procession of the Holy Spirit but to 'carry out' the will of the Father. The fact of the Son's being a servant of the Father does not only not lower Him but, on the contrary, it takes Him to the greatest heights. The position that He takes on the right hand of the Father is due to that fact. In the Holy Trinity, things do not 'function' in the way human societies function, full of pride and arrogance. The supreme attribute of God is simplicity which is expressed in the 'form' of humility. With the most detailed carrying out of the will of the Father, especially that of His dispensation, the Son seems to 'acquire' a most great power; now He can influence, in a way, the will of the Father. The Son can now 'persuade' the Father to send the Holy Spirit to the apostles. However, the Son Himself cannot cause the Holy Spirit to proceed.

Such an idea indicates sheer lack of knowledge of the mystery of the Holy Trinity. The begetting and the proceeding belong to the Father only. The Holy Spirit and the Son carry out the Will of the Father. This fact not only does not lower the Second and Third persons but it elevates them and renders them equal to the Father. Without them, the Father would not 'be able' to fulfill His wishes. According to the whole of the spirit of the Scriptures and of the Holy Tradition, the First Person begets the Son and causes the Holy Spirit to proceed by Him, equal to Himself. The idea of inequity among the Three Persons is inconceivable. Such a notion would cancel the unity of the Holy Trinity. The Holy Trinity provides us with a unique example of equality. Finally, the Holy Spirit undoubtedly proceeds from the First Person who has been called Father. From the above, it can be easily concluded that the Holy Spirit is equal to the other two Persons of the Holy Trinity. This is declared in a most explicit manner with the following words of the Creed.

who together with Father and Son is worshipped and together glorified;

We worship the Holy Spirit and praise It as much as we worship and glorify the Father and the Son. In this way, the above words of the Creed prove the *Filioque* absolutely wrong. The *Filioque* presents the Holy Spirit as inferior to the other two Persons of the Holy Trinity. It is strange that those people who added the *Filioque* did not notice these words of the Creed. The only explanation that one can find is that their understanding was confused, because the Creed is most explicit: the Holy Spirit 'is worshipped and glorified together with the Father and the Son' precisely because the Holy Spirit is con-substantial, and therefore equal to the other two Persons. The non-consubstantiality of even one of the Persons of the Holy Trinity would render the Holy Trinity non-existent. The existence of the Holy Trinity presupposes the con-substantiality and equality of the three persons.

It is true that what is said in the Creed about the Son as being con-substantial with the Father is not repeated here about the Holy Spirit. However, this is implied by the phrase 'who together with Father and Son is worshipped and together glorified'. It is not possible for a person to be worshipped and glorified together with the other two Persons and not to be con-substantial and equal to them.

The above argument can also be concluded from the position that the Holy Spirit has in the Holy Trinity. First of all, without it, we would not have Holy Trinity. We would have a *'Dyad'*, that is, a unity of two persons: the Father and the Son. How do the Three Persons fit in the Holy Trinity? We know that the Father is the source of divinity and that the Son is begotten from the Father and that that is the reason that the Son is con-substantial with Him. The Holy Spirit proceeds from the Father. That is why the Holy Spirit is con-substantial with the Father and the Son.

What does the word 'proceed' mean? In order for us to comprehend this proceeding from the Father, we must return to the Holy

Trinity once more. In this way, we might 'comprehend' the begetting of the Son from the Father as well. God always acts not as one person but as three persons, that is: in a Trinitarian fashion. For every act of God, the 'conception' of the plan and the volition for it belongs to the Father. The 'carrying out' of the plan belongs to the Son, while everything is 'performed' in the Holy Spirit. In this way, speaking in the most simplified manner about divine things, the Father 'would not be able to do anything' without His Son and the Holy Spirit. The above statement is made in order to indicate the importance of the existence of all three Persons of the Holy Trinity and in order for us to have a whole picture of God. This is the truth that is revealed in the Holy Bible, especially in the New Testament. That is: God is the God of Love, for the very reason that He is Trinity. The Father loves His Son more than anyone can imagine and the Holy Spirit proceeds from within the 'heart of His supreme Love'. In this way, the Father does not merely love the Holy Spirit but the Holy Spirit is His Love Itself.

All those who fight against the Holy Spirit, in fact are fighting against the Father's Love Itself and are doing away with the Holy Trinity. In every divine act, the volition belongs to the Father. Without the Son, however, nothing can be done. However, without the Holy Spirit, that which is done by the Logos cannot have life in it and it cannot 'function' at all.

The above reality is clear in all acts of God. In this way, let us say, we have the Father conceiving the idea for the creation of the world.

It is also evident that the Father wants to create the world. However, now He needs His Word or the Logos to proceed to the creation of the world. This reality is expressed by the phrase *'He said'* in the Bible. Behind this utterance, the existence of the Word or the Logos is concealed. St. John the evangelist tells us: 'In the beginning was the Word or the Logos'. In other words, the Logos existed before everything and even before time. St. John continues: 'and the Word was with God and the Word was God. He was in the beginning with God. All things were made through Him, **and without Him nothing was made that was made'** (John 1.1-3). Here we must stress the fact that the Greek text (which is the original) of the New Testament says διά (through) and not υπό (by). Therefore, the translation into English of 'by' is wrong. The right translation should be *'through'* and not 'by'. This is very important because the use of 'by' would mean that the creation was the exclusive act of the Son, which is not so. The Son is not the sole actor. The first one responsible for the creation of the world is the Father who 'conceived' and 'wanted' it to be created.

In a risky manner, let us compare this whole matter to what is happening with Man. When our hands make something, it is not the product of our hands only; it is the creation of the whole of Man. Our mind is responsible for conceiving the idea. There, inside our brain, the idea of our piece of work initially appeared. There (in our mind) the whole procedure took place of the conveyance of the idea to another centre of the brain in order for it to give, in its turn, the command to the hands. Ultimately, the piece of work cannot be attributed solely to either the brain or the hands but to the spirit of Man which rendered the piece of work into something beautiful, solid, useful and whatever other qualities that that piece of work might have. That is why we say that that piece of work is the work of the whole Man and not of a part of him. And when Man looks at his finished product and admires it and is so contented with it, it is not only his hands or his brain or even only his spirit (his imagination and so on), that admire it, but the whole Man. That is why the Bible tells us that after each day of the creation: 'And God saw that it was good'. And at the end of the creation: 'And God saw every thing that he had made, and, behold, it was very good' (Gen. 1.31). This means that God saw it as Trinity and not as one Person.

who spoke through the prophets

the prophets. Who are they? The English language does not help us find out who **the prophets** really are. The word **prophet** comes from the verb *prophesy* which means *foretell or predict the future*. Therefore, a prophet is generally considered to be the one who predicts the future. Unfortunately, this meaning predominates as a notion that exists in the minds of people, even the Greeks, in whose language the real meaning of *προφήτης* (prophet) is derived from *προ* and *φημί*. *Προ* (pro-), in this case, does not mean *before* (as it usually does), but it means *instead of (someone else)* or *representing (someone else)*. The word *φημί* (phimi) means *I speak*.

Therefore the two words actually mean, in this case, *I speak instead of someone else, or representing someone else*. It does not mean *I speak about (and therefore I disclose) things that are going to happen in the future*. It is with this meaning (the latter one) that most people mistakenly believe that a prophet is someone who predicts the future. If we believe something like that, then we do not distinguish a prophet from a seer or an oracle of Ancient Greece and other religions. A prophet is not a mere oracle. Among other things, he predicts the future, but he does not just do that. However, in doing that, he is most precisely a prophet.

However, let us see who a prophet really is. As we mentioned above, a prophet is someone who speaks instead of someone else. Here, this someone *else* is not anybody else. This *someone else* is God Himself. Therefore, the prophet speaks instead of God or as a representative of God. Whatever he says is not the product of his thinking or his philosophy. His words are not the fruit of his deliberation about God and His will. What he says is actually what God wants to disclose, tell or reveal to Man. Therefore, in a way, a prophet is the mouth of God. God does not have vocal cords. He speaks no human language. However, that does not mean that He is incapable of communicating with His creation and in this case with His supreme creation, which is Man.

Therefore, the prophets are actually the instruments of God in making His Will, His plans, His word, in general, known to His creation, Man. However, we should never think that the prophets are reluctant instruments of God who act unwillingly. It must be emphasized that they do not act in a compulsory fashion. They are chosen people, among the very few that remain steadfast to God's will, and they are in the service of God. They do not act mechanically either. God does not take their hands in order for them to write what He wants them to write. He does not open their mouth in order that they utter His words. Each prophet retains his individuality. That is why each prophet, depending on his education, character, philosophy, origin and even his times, writes or speaks in his own way. Each one of them has his own style. One can recognize that this kind of writing is of one particular prophet while that kind of writing is of some other prophet. And each prophet has a different message to give. However, all of them coincide on this: they all speak instead of God, telling us what God's will is and how God is. Among other things, they may predict certain things that are going to happen in the future, if this is necessary. Yet, again, this is not their mission. Prediction might be a part of a prophet's mission (and it usually is), if prediction is needed for the above purpose: the disclosure or the revelation of God's will and God's truths to us. The main purpose of the Old Testament's prophets' predictions was the coming of the Messiah. That is why we call those prophesies *Messianic*. There are really very few other predictions in the prophets other than the Messianic ones. And this is so because predictions are actually unnecessary if they do not serve the salvation of Man. Almost all predictions which do not serve that purpose are vain. And some-

The Creed

thing else: there are things that no Man may know. There are even things that even angels do not know. When Jesus is asked by His disciples John, Andrew and James: 'Tell us, when will these things be? and what *will be* the sign when all these things will be fulfilled?' (Mark 13.4), Jesus replied to them: 'Take heed that no one deceives you;' (Mark 13.5). Then He tells them: 'but of that day and hour no one knows, not even the angels in heaven, nor the Son, but only the Father. Take heed, watch and pray; for you do not know when the time is' (Mark 13.32-33).

However, we have not yet mentioned how they become prophets. As it is mentioned above, they are people devoted to God and especially in times when everybody has forgotten Him. So God chooses them from among so many people to serve Him in communicating with the rest. How do they actually become prophets? Here is how the Holy Spirit really 'works'. The Holy Spirit inspires them and they speak and they write. The Holy Spirit actually speaks through them. That is why we say: 'who spoke through the prophets'. Therefore, what is said or written by the prophets is actually what the Holy Spirit inspires them to say or write.

The Fathers and the saints of our Church and the Synods and everything else that is done in the Church with the action of the Holy Spirit Which acts in our Church and governs it, are nothing else but the power of God revealed in our world.

It is true that we classify the prophets. Some are great, others less so. However, each prophet serves the same purpose and is great because God is great and each one of them is a representative of God. Of course, the most important prophet for us Christians is St. John the Baptist. He is the greatest of all, because he was blessed by God to see the Messiah and even baptize Him. Prophets are not only the ones that we can find in the Old Testament, as some tend to believe. If that were the case, then Simeon, who held Jesus in his arms, would not be considered a prophet. But he is. And not only that, but St. Paul tells us that, in the early Christian Church, there were people who had this gift of prophecy. He says: 'And God has appointed these in the church: first apostles, second prophets, third teachers...'(1Cor.12.28). Therefore, those who believe that the prophets belong only to the Old Testament are wrong. Not only did God not cease to speak to Man through His prophets, but now He speaks through them in an even more authentic fashion. Now, He speaks through the members of His Church who are the Body of His Christ, His Son; of course, when they are genuine members of the Church. The highest authority speaking instead of God is the Ecumenical Council. In general, God speaks through His representatives, especially the bishops, who are the successors of the apostles. However, even they are genuine prophets only when they have the acceptance of the ecclesiastical conscience, which is the supreme authority in our Church, greater even than that of the Ecumenical Councils.

Article 9

In One, Holy, Catholic and Apostolic Church

✝

In

The phrase *I believe* is actually implied here as well. At the beginning of the Creed, we say 'I believe". That is not repeated within the Creed, yet it is implied every time that we begin a new article of the Creed. As we mentioned at the beginning of this book, the verb *believe* is always followed by the words 'in' or '*that.*' It is not possible for one to merely believe; one must believe *in* something or someone, or that something is so. Therefore, what follows here is the subject of our belief, along with the other subjects of our faith that we have encountered. In this case, the subject of our belief is the Church. Before we deal with the Church's attributive adjectives: one, holy, catholic and apostolic, we deem it necessary to deal with the Church Itself.

What is the **Church**? In Greek, the word for **Church** is *Εκκλησία (Ecclesia)*. Now, this word is a noun that comes from the verb *εκκαλώ (ekkalo)*, which means *I call people to gather together somewhere for some special purpose*. In Ancient Athens, *Ecclesia* was the gathering of the citizens of Athens to decide on a certain issue of public interest. This used to take place with an invitation which was carried out by a herald who went round the city calling everybody to the prescribed place for the above mentioned assembly.

When we, as Christians, use the word *Ecclesia*, we mean the gathering of the faithful at some special place for some kind of liturgical service or ceremony. Sometimes it is used as the place (the temple) in which we assemble.

Now, let us see what **Church** really is. Yes, the Church is the gathering of the faithful Christians together at a certain place. The actual gathering, though, is a mystical one. It **seems** to take place where it does. However, whatever that place is: a temple or a common building or even somewhere in the open, the gathering is the same for all. Let us see which place this is.

Just before His arrest and passion, Jesus was sitting down together with His disciples. Suddenly, He said to them: 'With fervent desire I have desired to eat this Passover with you before I suffer; for I say to you, I will no longer eat of it until it is fulfilled in the kingdom of God' (Luke 22.15-16). Jesus sent two of His disciples to meet the person who would offer the place and everything that was needed for the Passover. The place was the upper room of a house in Jerusalem (Mark 14.13-16).

In the evening, Jesus, together with His twelve disciples, gathered there. They all sat around the table that was prepared for them. (Mark 14.17). 'And as they were eating, Jesus took bread, blessed it, and broke *it*, and gave *it* to the disciples, and said, 'Take, eat; this is My Body'. Then He took the cup, and gave thanks, and gave *it* to them, saying, 'Drink from *it*, all of you. For this is My Blood of the new covenant, which is shed for many for the remission of sins' (Matt. 26. 26-28). After that, He told them: 'Do this in remembrance of Me' (Luke 22.19).

As was emphasized above, every moment, every movement, every word, every act of Jesus refers to us. His disciples are not just those that He had at that time; all of us who believe in Him, as our saviour and as our God, are also His disciples. When Jesus begs His Father for His disciples, we must know that He does not pray only for them but for us His eternal disciples as well. When we gather in church every Sunday, we do not actually go there. We go to that upper room where Jesus sat with His disciples. All of us are invited there. All of us participate in that mystical last supper. We actually receive from His own hands His Body and Blood. The bishop or priest that gives the Holy Communion is just a means. The one that is actually giving Jesus' Body and Blood to us is Jesus Himself. That is what **Church** is: the gathering round the same table of the Last, Mystical Supper; the supper without which we cannot have salvation. It is only through this that Man is united with God, the Real Life. In this way, we are freed from the realm of death, where we belonged after the fall, that is, the separation of Man from God.

The fact that we are united with Jesus, and therefore with God, brings us to the other dimension of the Church. And this is said because the Church has many aspects and dimensions. The Church is also the Body of Christ. From the moment we are united with Jesus, we belong to the Church, which is the Body of Jesus. Therefore, the faithful Christians are actually members of the Body of Christ.

One

Now, the **Church** cannot be many. There can only be **one.** How could the Body of Christ be more than one? Therefore, that is my belief, that there is only **one** Church. Of course, the Body that the Church is, is a Mystical one: you cannot see it with your fleshy eyes. You can only feel that you belong to it as the cell in our body feels that it belongs to the body where it is found.

There is a problem here, though. We know that there is the Orthodox Church, the Roman Catholic and the numerous Protestant churches. Could they all really be the Church? How could they be the Church since they are so many? How could the fact of their plurality, be reconciled with what we say in the Creed, **'one Church'**?

There have been many theories about this, the best known being this: that of a tree with branches. This theory says that: yes, the

Church is one, but as the tree has one trunk but many branches, so is it with the Church. It is one, but with many branches, which are the various denominations. If that was combined with what the deacon or the priest says just before the Creed is recited, then everything would be all right. The statement, which is actually a request, says: 'Let us love one another, that with **one mind** we may confess'. Is there such a thing: **one mind**? If there is, then the theory of the tree with the branches is right. Yet, things are not so at all. There is not **one mind**. And this is the actual problem. And there is not **one mind** because there is **no love** that unites us with one another.

This phrase **one mind** is very important for the question: Which, then, is the **one** Church that we believe in? And how can we be positive about it?

The **one** Church cannot be any other than the one that has remained steadfast to the original message that was handed down by the apostles to their successors, and from them to their successors and so on. That is why, as we shall see further on, this **one** Church is **apostolic**. Any deviation from the apostles' message is a deviation from the real Church. Anyone can go along and establish a 'church' of one's own, as in fact happens nowadays. However, that church is not **the** Church, the **one Church**. It is anything but that **one Church**.

When we say **the Orthodox Church,** we mean exactly that: The Church that retains the right faith. According to what was said above, this is the **one Church,** that we recite in the Creed. Of course, that does not mean that we should be proud of the fact, that because we are Orthodox we therefore have the privilege of belonging to the true **one Church.** The fact that I happened to be born into an Orthodox family and they baptized me, does not automatically make a truly living Orthodox Christian out of me. I might be worse than those who are not Orthodox. First of all, we should make sure that we know our faith. Secondly, we must try and enrich it and consolidate it. And thirdly, we must spread it: make it known to everybody, to the whole world. We are not justified if we keep it for ourselves. Actually, we must strive very hard so that one day the term *Orthodox* disappears because everybody will have the right faith and everybody will be called Christian without any attributive adjective before it.

Holy

The Church we believe in is **holy**. First of all, we must see what **holy** means. It means *perfect.* Someone or something that is holy is separated from everything that could have any stain of impurity or sinfulness. It means morally wholesome. It means the absolute absence of anything that can be characterized as bad or impure.

The question is: 'Can anybody or anything be **holy**?' The answer to this question is: only God can be holy. There is nothing and nobody who can be holy except God. How, then, do we call the Church **holy** and on which basis?

The Church is **holy** because Her founder is Jesus Christ, the Son of God, God Himself. As we said above, the Church is, among other things, the Body of Christ. However, the Body of Christ cannot be anything else but **holy**. The Church is **holy** because Her members are holy as well. How could the Body be holy but not Its members? How could the members of the Church be holy, though? Are they not human beings? And being a human being means that you are imperfect. And being imperfect means that you are not holy. There is a problem here. The problem is solved by finding out how Christians are holy or saintly. Of course, we call certain departed Christians saints who either sacrificed their lives for their faith or manifested an absolute devotion to their faith in this or that way. And we have their icons displayed in our church buildings. When we say saints or holy people, do we mean only those who were distinguished in their faith as we have just mentioned, or are all faithful Christians saintly or holy?

Let us see in the New Testament. St. Paul says in addressing the Christians of Rome: 'Among whom you also are the called of Jesus Christ; To all who are in Rome, beloved of God, called *to be saints*: Grace to you and peace from God our Father, and the Lord Jesus Christ' (Rom. 1.6-7). Addressing the Corinthians, he says: 'To the Church of God which is at Corinth, to those who are sanctified in Christ Jesus, called *to be* **saints**, with all who in every place call on the name of Jesus Christ our Lord, both theirs and ours' (I Cor. 1.2). In his epistle to the Philippians, he says: 'Greet every saint in Christ Jesus. The brethren who are with me greet you. All the saints greet you, but especially those who are of Caesar's household' (Phil.

4.21-22). And to the Colossians: 'To the saints and faithful brethren in Christ *who are* in Colosse' (Col. 1.2). In almost every one of his epistles, St. Paul calls all of the Christians **saints.** Now what does he mean by that? Does he mean that they are perfect like God? Are the Christians gods? Of course, they are not. Then why are they called saints? That does not mean that they are absolutely or partially perfect. No one can be perfect in any way except God. Then, why are they called saints? They are called **saints** because they are striving for perfection and they are on the way to it. There is also something else: they cannot be anything else but saints because they are members of the Church, which is the Body of Christ. Faithful Christians have decided to be separated from anything that is impure or morally filthy. This goes together with repentance. In Greek the word is **μετάνοια** (*metanoia*), which comes from two Greek words: **μετά** (*metà*) and **νους** (*nous*). The former does not mean *after* as it usually does; it implies *change* and the latter means *mind*. In other words, repentance **μετάνοια** (*metanoia*) means change of mind; a complete change of mind. The general philosophy and attitude of a Christian changes completely from the moment he or she is baptized. Baptism means the death of the old Man and the resurrection of the new Man, the Man in Christ. St. Paul says: 'I have been crucified with Christ; it is no longer I who live, but Christ lives in me; and the *life* which I now live in the flesh I live by faith in the Son of God, who loved me and gave Himself for me' (Gal. 2.20). However, this does not mean that this is only the exclusive privilege of St.

Paul. The same apostle says elsewhere: 'Or do you not know, that as many of us as were baptized into Christ Jesus were baptized into His death? Therefore we were buried with Him through baptism into death, that just as Christ was raised from the dead by the glory of the Father, even so we also should walk in newness of life. For if we have been united together in the likeness of His death, certainly we also shall be *in the likeness* of His resurrection, knowing this, that our old man was crucified with *Him*, that the body of sin might be done away with, that we should no longer be slaves of sin. For He who has died has been freed from sin. Now if we died with Christ, we believe that we shall also live with Him, knowing that Christ, having been raised from the dead, dies no more. Death no longer has dominion over Him. For in *the death* that He died, He died to sin once for all; but *the life* that He lives, He lives to God. Likewise you also reckon yourselves to be dead indeed to sin, but alive to God in Christ Jesus our Lord' (Rom. 6.3-11). St. Paul is so clear about what we are trying to establish that no explanations are really necessary.

catholic

The Church is also **catholic**. There is a misunderstanding here. Many people think that **catholic** is the church that is governed by the Pope. The error here lies in the fact that the papal church is actually called Roman Catholic. And even the word *catholic* that is used

The Creed

there does not represent the true meaning, as one can gather from what is going to follow.

What does the word **catholic** mean, then? The meaning of the word, as it is used in the Creed, is multi-dimensional. One of the meanings is that the Church (to which it refers) embraces everyone and everything. It is not without significance that the crucified Jesus has his arms wide open. Up there, on the Cross, He beckons to everybody to approach Him and He is ready to embrace anybody who is willing to accept the salvation He offers. He makes a start with the robber, the one crucified with Him, whom He accepts in His Kingdom. Nobody is excluded from His work of dispensation and salvation. The Church embraces everybody no matter what race, what colour, what nationality one is. The Church embraces every place. All the globe is invited. And not only the globe; all of the universe. When Man will find himself traveling in space, there, as well, the Church will stretch out her arms to embrace the space-travellers of tomorrow. The Church wishes to embrace also all people no matter what religion or what ideology they belong to. That is why the Church is not a religion. The Church is the New Creation, the New Jerusalem, the New Israel, the Unique Way leading to the Kingdom of God. It is not a religion because Jesus Christ is not the founder of a religion, but He is the incarnate Son of God. He is the only one that can save Man from real death, which is the separation of Man from God, the true Life.

The Church is **catholic** from another aspect as well. The Church embraces all time. What does that mean? The Church embraces the past, the present and the future. It embraces all those who lived in the past and were united with Jesus Christ, all those who live in the present and belong to His Body, that is: His Church, and all those who will live in the future and will be united in His Body, that is: the Church. All those who were crucified along with Christ and buried their old selves, all those who do that today and all those who will be doing that up to the end of all time and of this world, are part of Christ's Church. Of course, it is easy to understand about the past and the present; but how is it possible for the Church to embrace the future as well? The future has not come; how is it possible to speak about it as if it were present? We have dealt with that. Within the Church, we have the transformation of time. This means that, in Church, the past and the future are dissolved in the perpetual present. In Church, we have the taste of eternity, where there is no time. The Church lives in the eighth day. We all know that the week has seven days. That is the cycle of the week. Where does the eighth day fit in, then? That is what it is all about. It does not fit in because it belongs to a new era: the 'epoch' of the Kingdom of God. For the Church, this life, as well as time, is transient. Both were created by God in order to fulfill a purpose (the purpose of the salvation of Man), and then they will fade away. Everything and everybody will return to where they were separated from: eternity. The eighth day is exactly that, the beginning of eternity. That is why it does not fit in

The Creed

the cycle of the seven days of the week. The eighth day is Sunday, which in Greek is called **Κυριακή** *(Kyriaki),* which means the *day of the Lord.* It is the day that Jesus was resurrected from the dead. For the Jews it was (and it still is) Saturday (the Sabbath), the seventh and last day of the week, the day that they celebrate and which they devote to God. It was not a coincidence that Jesus was resurrected in the early hours of Sunday (one of the Sabbaths). The day of the resurrection denotes the beginning of the new era in Man's HISTORY. It is actually the end of History and the beginning of the new HISTORY of Man, the one that is leading Man into Eternity and the Kingdom of God.

St. Matthew says: 'Now after the Sabbath, as the first *day* of the week began to dawn,...'(Matt.28.1). The Greek text, which is the original, says: *'οψέ δε σαββάτων, τη επιφωσκούση εις μίαν σαββάτων...',* which means: 'After Saturday, as one of the Sabbaths was just dawning ...' St. Mark says: 'Now when the Sabbath was past...'(Mark 16.1). In Greek, the text says: *'Και διαγενομένου του σαββάτου...',* which means: 'As the Sabbath had passed...' St. Luke says: 'Now on the first *day* of the week, very early in the morning...'(Luke 24.1) In Greek, the text says: *'τη δε μια των σαββάτων όρθρου βαθέος...',* which means: 'and on one of the sabbaths, when it was early dawn...' and St. John says: 'Now on the first *day* of the week..' (John 20.1). In Greek, the text says: *'Τη δε μια των σαββάτων..',* which means: 'On one of the sabbath days..'. All of the gospels agree on the phrase: *'one of the sabbaths'*. But then, how can there be more than one sabbath? We know that Saturday, like every other day, is just one. There cannot be more than one of each of the days of the week. How can we then speak about more than one sabbath? The explanation is what we have just mentioned: that this day, the day on which Jesus was resurrected, does not belong to the regular cycle of the week and therefore it does not belong to time itself. That is why there are other *'dimensions'* within the **Church.** That is why the present tense is predominant in our liturgical practice. For instance, on Good Thursday, we chant: 'Today He who has hung the world on waters is being crucified'. The crucifixion, as well as the resurrection and every event of Jesus' life, is seen as happening now. We can see Him being born, being in the Temple mystifying the archpriests there at the age of twelve, being baptized by John the forerunner, kneeling and praying in the garden of olives, suffering all of those torments and finally being crucified on the wooden Cross. We can see Him being buried in the tomb, being resurrected and appearing before His disciples, ascending into Heaven and sitting at the right hand of His Father. All these events are not seen by us as past events of a person who lived two thousand years ago and who founded a religion which poses as one of the major religions of the world. Our faith is the only Way that can lead Man into the Kingdom of God.

and apostolic

and. In addition to Its being One, Holy and Catholic, the Church is apostolic as well. What does **apostolic** mean? It is obvious. The Church derives its faith from the apostles. They were the ones who were with Jesus all the time: from the moment He started His work of our salvation up to the moment that they lost Him from their sight as He was ascending into Heaven.

Why are they called apostles? The word is actually from Greek *απόστολος (apostolos)* which comes from the Greek verb: αποστέλλω **(apostello)**, which means *I dispatch* or *send*. Just before Jesus ascended into Heaven, He spoke to His disciples saying: 'All authority has been given to Me in heaven and on earth. Go therefore and make disciples of all the nations, baptizing them in the name of the Father and of the Son and of the Holy Spirit, teaching them to observe all things that I have commanded you; and, lo, I am with you always, *even* to the end of the age' (Matt. 28.18-20). His disciples were sent by Him to bring the Gospel to the whole world. That is why they are also called apostles: the ones sent by Him. And that is why the Church is called apostolic: because it was founded and taught by the apostles. The apostles, being devoted to the Lord, went out into the world and brought the message of salvation through Christ. They passed on their mission and blessing that they received from the Holy Spirit to their successors, and they to theirs and so on. That is the *apostolic succession*. That is why we call the Church **apostolic.**

Church

We have already referred to what the Church really is. However, the Church cannot be defined with just one definition. The Church is many things: She is the *building with Jesus Christ as its foundation stone*. She is *the ark in which Man can be saved from the flood of destruction of this world.* She is *the branches of the vineyard which is Christ Himself.* She is *the bride of the bridegroom, who is Christ.* She is *the harbour where Man can find peace, quiet and safety.* She is *the Upper Room where the Last and Mystical Supper took place.* She is many other things that mean the Body of salvation. The present Body of the Church is in two stages: the heavenly or triumphant Church and the earthly or struggling Church. The Church is *a medical centre* where we sinners receive the proper medicine to put on our wounds, as St. John Chrysostom says (PG 53,22). St. John also says that the Church 'is a spiritual fair and a medical centre for the souls' (PG 53,293), it is 'the Zion and the Mount' (PG 55.130), 'the house of God' (PG 56.29-30), 'the mother of everybody and the gathering in it and the fair of all the heavenly and earthly' (PG 56.97), 'the common and main house of everybody, where all our *property* and our hopes lie' (PG 57.384), 'the fair of angels' (PG 58,508), 'declared as stronger than Heaven' (PG 58.535), 'preferable to Heaven and earth' (PG 58,702), 'the one that is made up of the blood and water that came out of the crucified dead body of Christ' (PG 59,463), 'a fortress against the devil' (PG 60,148), 'the union of previously divided Men' (PG 61,228), 'The place of archangels, angels, the Kingdom of God, Heaven Itself' (PG 61,313), 'a spiritual bath, where one can get rid of all stains through repentance' (PG 61,510) 'the fullness of Christ, because the fullness of the head is the body and the fullness of the body is its head' (PG 62,26), 'the pillar of the whole world' (PG 62,554), 'harbour and paradise. The Church is greater than the ark because the ark accepted in it animals and kept them as animals, whereas the Church accepts the animals and changes them' (PG 49,336)', 'higher than Heaven and broader than the earth, never getting older' (PG 52,402).

According to the same church father, the church never ceases being fought against and never ceases being victorious. All the powers of Hades cannot prevail over Her. Those who fight against Her destroy themselves while the Church becomes even stronger. Those who wage war against Her consume their own strength, while they contribute for our trophy to be of even greater splendour' (PG 52,449). The Church was built with many sacrifices and dangers. An assistant and ally was the invincible power of the One who said: 'on this rock, I will build My church' (Matt.16,18).

We owe a lot to St. Luke the evangelist, who wrote the Acts of the Apostles. If he had not written this book, we would not have the History of the early Church. We would not know the life of the Church as it began from the illumination of the Holy Spirit on Pentecost up to the travels of St. Paul to Rome and his discussions with the Jews of Rome. It was actually in the providence of God that Luke wrote this book. In this way, we can see very clearly that the Church is really what we have said up to here and even more than that. We can see the hand of God leading and guiding His Church. We can see that the Church has not been established by human powers but by the Heavenly powers and in essence by Jesus Christ the incarnate Son of God.

Article 10

I confess one baptism for the forgiveness of sins

†

Confess. Here, this verb does not have its common meaning which is: *I acknowledge my sins and I tell them to my confessor in order for him to give me absolution from them.* The meaning of this verb here is: *I solemnly and with courage declare my faith in something.*

Therefore, **I confess one baptism** means: I declare my faith in **one baptism**. The stress here is, of course, on the number **one**. There cannot be more than **one** baptism. Yet, there is another stress here: on **baptism**. There cannot be any true Christian without him/her been baptized. Why? Because without baptism one cannot bury his/her own old Man in order for the new Man to be resurrected from the tomb which is symbolized by the water of the baptismal font. And this is done in the name of the Father, of the Son and of the Holy Spirit. This is actually the command of Jesus to His disciples just before His ascension into Heaven: 'Go therefore, and make disciples of all the nations, baptizing them in the name of the Father and of the Son and of the Holy Spirit' (Matt. 28.19).

The sacrament of baptism is preceded by the catechesis. During that, the priest asks the one that is about to be baptized to reject Satan and even spit on him. Then he asks him to declare that he accepts Jesus Christ. Finally, the one who is about to be baptized is asked to recite the Creed. All these things are nothing else but a confession of his/her faith. Now, the one to be baptized is ready to accept the sacrament of baptism, which is the initiation of someone into the Church. Without it, one cannot say that one is a member of the Church, no matter how great his faith in Christ might be.

for the forgiveness of sins

forgiveness: In Greek this word has two different meanings: one of them is: συγχώρησις (synhôresis) and the other one is: άφεσις (afesis). The latter one means: *absolution*; the former one comes from the verb συγχωρώ *(synhorô)*, which is composed of two parts: συν + χωρώ (syn + horô). The verb χωρώ *(horô)* is related to the noun: χώρος *(horos)* which means *space*. The conjunction συν *(syn),* which is similar to the English (actually Latin) prefix *con*, in this case, means *together.* Therefore, actually, the verb συγχωρώ *(synhorô)* means something like: *I take someone together with me into the same space.* And this space is in fact nothing else but *the heart.* Therefore, the actual meaning of it is: *I take you into* *my heart.* Actually, that is how the true Christian is: He/she takes everybody into his/her heart. A true Christian *συγχωρεί (synhori) forgives* everybody, friends and enemies. In fact, a true Christian has no enemies. He imitates Jesus, who, from up there, from the Cross, He forgives (that is: He takes into His great heart) even those who have crucified Him.

The above is one of the two main meanings of **forgiveness** or **remission.** The one which applies here, however, is that of *άφεσις (afesis),* which means *absolution* or *remissions of sins.* This noun comes from the verb: *αφίημι (afiemi),* which means: *I let something go.* In our case here: *I let sins go.* Therefore, one whose sins are let go, one is actually free from those sins.

sins. What are they? First of all, there is actually **one** sin. The ones that are called sins are actually the product of that major sin.

Let us first turn to the Greek language in which these things were originally expressed. In Greek, the word for *sin* is *αμαρτία (amartia).* This word comes from the verb *αμαρτάνω (amartano).* In Ancient Greek, this verb used to mean: *I fail in my target,* that is: *I aim, I shoot, and I fail to hit my target.* Therefore, *αμαρτία (amartia)* used to mean *failure of a very great significance.*

Another etymology of the word is: *α + μέρος* (a + meros). The former is a particle of negative significance. It means absence of what the other part of the word is. The latter, in this case *μέρος (meros),* means *a part* or *place.* Therefore, the meaning of *αμαρτία (amartia)* of this etymology is: *not taking part in.*

Both of the above etymologies of the word *αμαρτία* (amartia) fit its theological meaning. With the first etymology, *αμαρτία* (amartia) is Man's failure to attain divinity. Man *aimed at the target of divinity and failed*. Why did he fail, though? He failed because he did not try to attain divinity in accordance with the plan of God. Man was created by God in order for Man to become god by grace. When God 'decided' to create Man, He decided to create him in His image and likeness. Now, the former means that Man was created with all the attributes of God: freedom, logos and so many others, pre-eminently the fact that Man was created to be a person as God is three Persons. The likeness of God with which Man was created means the potentiality of Man to become god himself by grace. One might ask: 'why then was Man unsuccessful in his attempt to become god, since Man was created to become god?' The fault does not lie with the fact that Man tried to become god, but with the fact that he tried it prematurely. Man was not yet ready to become god. This potentiality of his to become god, does not mean that Man was to decide when and how that would be achieved. Therefore, the deification of Man, which is the end of Man's evolution, according to the plan of God, becomes Man's *αμαρτία* (amartia), that is: sin. This failure meant his separation from God. And this, by the way, is the meaning of the same word *αμαρτία* that is: not taking part in the Life that God is. That meant, that now Man would 'live' in a new kind of existence, which, in one word, is described as death. This actually is the real death. The other death that we usually refer to is biological or natural or physical death. The latter is nothing else but the outcome of the real death: the separation of Man from God, who is Life Itself. Now, this new kind of existence is not the creation of God. And that is so because it is not a positive existence; it is a negative one. And God is not the creator of any negative existence. And who then is the 'creator' of it? It is Satan's 'creation'. Death became a reality, a negative one, when Satan was separated from His creator, God. Being away from God, who is Life, a new kind of existence was 'created'. This was followed by everything that is evil. Evil, along with death, is not the creation of God for the same reason: God is not the creator of anything negative. Neither evil nor death, are positive things. They are absolutely negative. This means that they exist but in the same way that minus (-) in Mathematics exists. It does not mean anything positive but negative. It does not add up to anything. On the contrary, it takes away. Evil in general is either the absence of everything positive or the opposite of it. All forms of evil are like that. Darkness is the absence of light; misery is the absence of happiness; stress, anxiety and all situations of their kind are the absence of peace, and so on. There is no end to these pairs. Every form of good has its own counterpart on the evil side. Naturally, God did not create the world that contains evil. God forbid! However, God created His spiritual world with freedom. Therefore, some of His spiritual creation, acting freely, decided to go away from Him. If they had not, then evil would not exist. However, as they decided to go away from God, these negative conditions, which we call evil, were the outcome.

Man was found in this situation by listening to Satan instead of obeying God and following God's plan for Man. That is why Man failed in his attempt to become god by grace and that is why Man was found in death. And that is exactly the plan of God of Oikonomia (dispensation) through Jesus Christ, His Son to save us from this most grave situation. And this is done with baptism, which should take place only once.

Article 11

I await the resurrection of the dead

✝

I await

When one waits for someone, one remains at a certain place and does not leave that place until the person that one wants to see arrives. To wait for somebody is a common experience. We all happen to wait for someone. To await someone or something is something else. It implies some kind of feeling. It involves more than just waiting. In Greek, the word that is used is *προσ-δοκώ (prosdoko)*, which means *I expect*. When you *expect* something to happen, first of all, you believe that it will happen. You have a certain kind of knowledge that makes you think that the thing you expect will really happen. And that is the case here. However, there is something more involved here. There is something more than expectation in this case. It is something that I very fervently wish to take place the sooner the better. Therefore, the translation *I look for* that certain English versions have from the Greek προσδοκώ instead of *I await*, is more suitable for this last meaning. The true Christian, the one who is a genuine member of the Body of Jesus Christ, wishes most fervently that that day of the resurrection take place now, if possible.

the resurrection

Awaiting the resurrection is a kind of expectation. We know that it will happen. It is a matter of time, as the common expression goes, before it occurs. In fact, this expectation is something like saying: 'we really wonder how this has not occurred yet'. This expectation is not a mere expectation; it is an experience. We live it out. As Christians, we live with it. It is as if it is happening every moment of our lives.

As we mentioned above, in our Church, we have a transformation of time. Time is not divided into past, present and future. Past and future are 'dissolved' into the everlasting present. The eighth day that we mentioned above is not a regular day. It is the time that is translated into eternity. It is the first step that we take from the space-time world into eternity. Therefore, this expectation that we have about the resurrection is not the same kind of expectation that we have about other things that we place in the future. This expectation is a live experience. It does not belong to the future. It belongs to the present. It is as if the resurrection has already taken place.

Now, what kind of resurrection do we expect? Is it something like the resurrection of the son of the widow of Nain? Or even of Lazarus? Nothing of the kind. It is THE resurrection, the model of which is given by Jesus Himself. He was buried in the tomb and when the myrrh-bearing women sought Him, they could not find Him. He was not in the tomb. The evangelists do not tell us how He was resurrected. Maria could not recognize Him when she first saw Him. Therefore, the resurrected body is not exactly the same as the buried one. However, finally she recognized Him from His voice and other unknown to us features. It was Him. She had no doubt that it was Him. He appeared before His disciples while the doors of the upper room where they were were firmly shut. That means that the body that we shall have will know no obstacles. It will be a body but of another nature. It will have all the potentialities that we can think of. It can eat (Luke 24.41-43), without food being necessary for it to survive like the one we have. It will not change and therefore it will not decay or wear or get older or suffer any illness or pain and of course it will not know death. Yet, it will be a body (Luke 24.36-40). If we say that it will be something spiritual, we are wrong. Actually, the heretics think little of the body. The body is sacred because it was created by God. In fact, God created it first and then the spirit in Man. And something else: what kind of resurrection is it if it is not the resurrection of the body? And this brings us to the next phrase:

of the dead.

What do we mean by that? The word **dead** here is used because that is what Man's experience is when someone leaves this world of space-time. We see our relative or friend lying there without his heart beating at all and, of course, without his body functioning in any way. And if the body is left, it will disintegrate and start smelling. It is buried and after some time, only the bones are left. That is the experience that we have of our fellow-men leaving this world. Some people (not real Christians, of course) think or even believe that that is the end of Man. There is nothing further than that. The grave is the end of Man for them.

It is exactly that which we, Christians, do not believe. We do not believe in the extinction or disappearance of Man with his biological death. On the contrary, we believe that that is the real beginning of true life for Man. Man is 'born' into another kind of life in eternity. It is an unknown kind of life to Man. However, Christians have some experience, some kind of taste of this eternal life that we are entering as soon as our body stops functioning in this world of space-time.

Now, here there is a problem. When will the resurrection take place? The answer to this question is very difficult, yet, at the same time, very simple. No matter how strange this may sound, it is the truth. It is extremely difficult for one who is accustomed to living in space and time to comprehend fully how life is in eternity where there is no space and no time. It is certain that the resurrection will

The Creed

take place in time for those who will be living in this world of space and time. However, this is not so for those who have departed. This is because, once we depart from this world, we do not live in space and time but in eternity. Therefore, the resurrection takes place in eternity for those who have departed. That is the reason why St. Paul says that the dead will be resurrected **first** and **then** the ones who will be living in this world.

There is something else that we must point out here. Of course, St. Paul as well as the Creed here seems to divide Men into the living and the dead. That does not mean that either of them think that the real living people are us and that those who have departed are really dead. They both use these words because that is the way people are accustomed to think. In fact, the Church Itself calls the ones who have departed **κεκοιμημένοι** *(kekoimemenoi)*, meaning *the sleeping ones*. That is why the place where they are buried is not called **νεκροταφείο** *(necrotafeio)*, which means a place where the dead are buried (a graveyard) but it is called **κοιμητήριο** *(koimeterio)*, which means *the place in which the ones who are sleeping are found*. It is from that Greek word that the English word *cemetery* is derived from.

The Early Church was characterized by the anticipation of the Second Advent of Christ. And that is why we can see this great enthusiastic element of the first Christians. This was that made them so courageous and so decisive in sacrificing their lives for their faith in Jesus. In fact, this should be so all the time, even after two thousand years. This is so because the time that has elapsed since then is nothing for our Church which lives in the eighth day, which is the beginning of eternity, where there is no time and space.

Article 12

and the life of the age to come. Amen

✝

and the life

Life. What is **life**? Most people think of life as it is commonly known. Actually, Biology studies all organisms that have life in them. They are called living organisms. Of course, there are many kinds of them. They are divided into different realms: of the animals, the plants, the fungi, the micro-organisms, the protozoa, the sea life (fishes etc.), the birds and the serpents. Therefore, we have the respective individual sciences of: Zoology, Botany, Mycology, Microbiology, Ichthyology and Marine Life Biology, Ornithology and Herpetology. All of these sciences deal with living organisms, that is, organisms that have life in them. Naturally, in each of these areas, life presents different kinds of traits. That is one of the reasons that we have all of these different sciences.

Man belongs to the realm of animals. Anthropology is not actually a science that belongs to Biology. It is a broader science examining the phenomenon *άνθρωπος (anthropos)*, that is: Man from all aspects. As a biological living organism, Man belongs to the realm of animals. He belongs to the family of mammals, that is: the animals where the mother nourishes her young with milk which is produced by her mammary glands.

This is the life that most people know and accept. They do not accept any other kind of life beyond this biological one. Let us see, though, if they are right or wrong. Where has this life first appeared? Scientists have some kind of explanation about that. They cannot explain the origin of this first life, though. However, they know for certain that nothing can come from nothing. Everything must have some cause or origin. Science must have the humility to declare her limits. Science can deal only with things that can be observed, examined and analyzed. They use Mathematics as their own language of expressing their findings. Science is an admirable occupation of Man. However, it is not everything. It helps Man find the truths that are there in the natural world. It can also help Man make his life more comfortable with technology. Scientists, however, are not in a position to enter and examine any area beyond that. However, **there is** an area beyond that: the area of metaphysics. It is there where Philosophy, Theology and other similar disciplines find truths that Science would never dream of finding. The reason for that is that in metaphysics, no scientific observations or experimentation or scientific analyses can be made and no Mathematics can be used. However, the above-mentioned disciplines deal with that area most solemnly with findings of their own that a scientist would never dream of achieving. It is in this area where real Life can be found. It is this Life that is the real cause of life that biology examines. Without this Life, no life would exist, not even inanimate things. Everything has its origin in this Life. Therefore, it is in the area of metaphysics that Man can find solutions to his problems that Science is finding itself incapable of solving.

This Life is not easy for Man to find. Jesus says: 'Because narrow is the gate and difficult is the way, which leads to life, and there are few who find it' (Matt.7.14). What is this life that is so difficult for Man to find? First of all, it is eternal. Jesus says: 'And these will go away into everlasting punishment, but the righteous into eternal life' (Matt. 25.46) and 'It is easier for a camel to go through the eye of a needle than for a rich man to enter the kingdom of God' (Mark 10.25), where there is real eternal Life. And what is this Life? Jesus replies: 'I am the bread of Life' (John 6.35). Jesus also says: 'And this is the will of Him who sent Me, that everyone who sees the Son and believes in Him may have everlasting life; and I will raise him up at the last day' (John 6.40). Who is this Life? Jesus is most clear about that: 'I am the way, the truth, and the Life' (John 14.6).

Of course, there is a choice for us to make: this transient life or that everlasting Life? Jesus is very clear about that as well: 'And he who does not take his cross and follow after Me is not worthy of Me.

He who finds his life will lose it, and he who loses his life for My sake will find it' (Matt. 10.38-39). Jesus uses the word *life* in two different ways: the former is this transient life and the latter is the Life that He is, the everlasting Life. We must make our choice: the first or the second. If we choose the first, then we lose the second. What does it mean to choose between the two? Of course, it does not mean that we should seek to put an end to this transient life. This life, no matter how transient it is, has a purpose in the plan of God for our salvation. It is within this life that we can attain the eternal one. It was created by God, so that, in His Providence, we might grasp the opportunity to be saved through Jesus Christ. It is within the framework of this life that we can attain true Life. However, to be able to do that, we must realize how transient this life is and do whatever is necessary to attain the other One, the everlasting Life. What we need to do in order to attain the everlasting Life is said by Jesus. We must bear our cross, whatever that is, and follow Christ. To follow Him, we must obey His commandments, which are included in one: 'Love your neighbour like yourself'. Our neighbour is anyone of our fellow-men who is in any kind of need. We do not have to seek and find Jesus; He is in front of us; He is anyone who is in this or that kind of need: one who is dying out of thirst or hunger; one who has no clothes to put on; one who is in hospital or prison; one who is fed up with life and wants to put an end to it, and so on.

Furthermore, when we are faced with the choice of either confessing or not confessing faith in Jesus, we are actually faced with choosing either this transient life or the everlasting One. We cannot enter the Kingdom of God, the abode of the everlasting Life, without bearing a cross on our shoulders.

of the age to come

of the age to come. In the original Greek text, we have *και ζωήν του μέλλοντος αιώνος* which means: *'and life of the future age'*. Of course, the idea is similar; the age to come is nothing else but the future one. We refer to the Greek text to emphasize the idea of *future*. It is true that this life belongs to the future. However, we must stress the fact that this applies to us who live in the present age of this present life. In fact, the age to come is nothing else but the eighth day which we mentioned above. This eighth day has already started and that is why we already have a taste of eternity. The future as well as the past are dissolved, in a way, into the present. There is a perpetual present for us. When the reference is to us, it means those who really believe in Jesus, bear our cross and follow Him all the days of our life. Yes, in this Church, this miraculous reality is evident: the transformation of time. The past, the present and the future become one: an everlasting present. Therefore, the age to come, which the Creed mentions here, is actually here. It has already started and it will be fulfilled with the general resurrection. The resurrection will not be an event in time but of the age to come, of eternity. All those who have departed from this life belong to eternity and not to space and

The Creed

time. Therefore, all those who have departed are resurrected in eternity. The present tense (are) is used here to emphasize this fact: that for those who belong to eternity, these things (like the resurrection) take place in eternity. Therefore, there is no expectation for them but just the anticipation of the end of this present age.

Amen

Amen: This is a Hebrew word. It has several meanings and uses. One of these is the one that Jesus makes at the beginning of some of His statements, sometimes using it twice. In those cases, it means *verily*. However, at the end of a statement or at the end of a prayer, it means: *let it be so*. In this case, as well as in similar cases, it is used to conclude what has just been said and, in a way, seal it with the absolute approval of the one who has said what was said. Therefore, in this case, *Amen* means: What I have just said about what I believe in is true and there is no doubt about that. In a way, it is as if I say: *I firmly believe in what I have just stated.*

EPILOGUE

✝

The Creed is all the fundamental articles of our faith. Our faith is in the Holy Trinity, that is: the three Persons of: the Father, the Son and the Holy Spirit.

More analytically, the first Person, the Father, is the source of divinity. The second Person, the only-begotten Son of the Father, begotten before all ages, is not created by the Father, like us and like all creation in general, visible and invisible. He is begotten, that is: He comes from the same essence as the Father and that is why He is considered as consubstantial with the Father. We also believe that this second Person is the actual creator of everything and everybody. Naturally, the Father made everything but it was through him, the Son, that they were made. This is emphasized by St. John, the apostle of Jesus, the evangelist. He says at the very beginning of his gospel: 'In the beginning was the Word (the Logos), and the Word was with God, and the Word was God. He was in the beginning with God. All things were made through Him, and without Him was nothing was made that was made' (John 1.1-3). This same Person is Light. He is actually the Light. The Creed says: 'Light from Light'. As He is the only-begotten Son and therefore consubstantial with the Father, He is Light from the Light who is, of course, the Father. That He is also the Light, is made evident again from St. John: 'That was the true Light which gives light to every man coming into the world' (John 1.9). Jesus Himself says: 'I am the light of the world. He who follows Me shall not walk in darkness, but have the light of life' (John 8.12) and 'I have come *as* a light into the world, that whoever believes in Me should not abide in darkness' (John 12.46). St. Paul, on his way to Damascus, first met Jesus as light: 'As he journeyed he came near Damascus, and suddenly a light shone around him from heaven. Then he fell to the ground, and heard a voice saying to him, 'Saul, Saul, why are you persecuting Me?' And he said, 'Who art You, Lord?' Then the Lord said, 'I am Jesus whom you are persecuting. It *is* hard for you to kick against the goads.' (Acts 9.3-5). A reflection of this Light passes on to His disciples (and us, their successors, if we are really His disciples). Jesus Himself tells His disciples: 'You are the light of the world. A city that is set on a hill cannot be hidden. Nor do they light a lamp and put it under a basket, but on a lamp-stand, and it gives light to all *who are* in the house. Let your light so shine before men, that they may see your good works and glorify your Father in heaven' (Matt. 5.14-16). The prophet Simeon was able to recognize in the baby Jesus 'the light to bring the revelation to the Gentiles' (Luke 2.32). That this would be the case, is proven later in the life of the early Church: 'For so the Lord has commanded us: 'I have set you as a light to the Gentiles, that you should be for salvation to the ends of the earth' (Acts 13.47). St. Paul tells us: 'For you were once darkness, but now you are light in the Lord. Walk as children of light' (Eph. 5.8). St. John warns and complains: 'He who believes in Him is not condemned; but he who does not believe is condemned already, because he has not believed in the name of the only begotten Son of God. And this is the condemnation that the light has come into the world, and men loved darkness rather than light, because their deeds were evil.' (John 3.18-19). Jesus also warns us: 'Take heed therefore that the light which is in you is not darkness' (Luke 11.35). Jesus explains: 'The lamp of the body is the eye. If therefore your eye is good, your whole body will be full of light. But if your eye is evil, your whole body will be full of darkness. If therefore the light that is in you is darkness, how great is that darkness!' (Matt. 6.22-23).

Jesus is the true Light because He is true God from true God. Since He is the Son of the Father, begotten and not made, and therefore, consubstantial with the Father, He cannot be anything else but true God, because He is of the same essence as the Father.

Among other things, the Son is the Person who obeys the will of His Father. The Father loves humanity and therefore, the Son does the same. This love is expressed in many ways. One of these is the favour that God shows to us. The favour in this case consists of the fact that God decides to show Man His willingness to accept Man back into His Kingdom. Therefore, for the sake of Man, the Son humiliates Himself to the utmost and takes on our nature along with His divine nature. This *kenosis* (emptying of Himself) constitutes the greatest humiliation that God could undergo. The creator takes on the nature of one of His creatures: Man. This shows His supreme attribute which is nothing else but SIMPLICITY. This simplicity is what makes the unity of the three Persons become a reality and thus a Trinity, which means One God. Without this absolute simplicity, we would have three gods. It is within this attribute, SIMPLICITY, that His other attributes have meaning. Freedom has a place inside simplicity; love has a place inside freedom; justice has a place inside love; purity has a place inside justice and so on. In this way, all of God's attributes are to be sought within this supreme attribute: SIMPLICITY. God is simplicity and every and each Person of the Holy Trinity is simplicity. This is shown by the Father in begetting His Son. It is also shown by the Son by obeying His Father and emptying Himself in taking on our nature. And the Holy Spirit is actually the spirit of SIMPLICITY itself. This is shown in all of the Holy Spirit's manifestations.

We can see that all three Persons take part in the work of **Οικονομία** (dispensation). The Father has planned it because He wanted His chosen creation, Man, to return to Him and to His Kingdom. The Son performs His Father's plan. And the Holy Spirit completes it and governs the outcome of the Son's work. Everything is made for the sake of Man. The salvation that is offered to Man

The Creed

had to follow a certain plan, the plan of the Father. The Son had to take on the nature of Man, along with His divine Nature. Therefore, He had to be conceived. This conception could not be a normal one. If the Saviour of the world was conceived in the same fashion that every Man is conceived, then He would have the same stigma as every and each one of us. This would mean that He would need to be saved from the stigma Himself. In other words, He would need a saviour Himself. There is something else: the stigma is that of Sin. Sin means the separation of Man from God. However, how could the Son, who is God, be separated from God, that is, Himself? That is impossible. There is something else, too. Before the fall, the Son of God *συνήν τω Αδάμ* (which means that *the Son of God co-existed with Adam*). With the fall, Man loses this co-existence and this is the greatest misfortune that Man suffers by the fall. Actually, with the dispensation that is carried out by the Son, this co-existence is realized again with the Son's sacrifice and with the Communion of His Body and Blood. With this re-union, Man can achieve the state in which Man co-existed with the Son and thus belong to the Kingdom of God.

The above-mentioned plan of the Father is carried out in the Person of the Son with the work of the Holy Spirit. The latter chooses the most pure woman. This corresponds to Satan's choice of Eve to bring about the fall of Man. Satan chooses a spiritually weak woman who has developed pride and conceit inside her soul and who is ready to disobey her Creator. The Holy Spirit approaches a woman, the second Eve, the Virgin Mary who is the exact opposite of the first Eve. The Virgin Mary is full of humility and obedience towards God. It is through these two, the Holy Spirit and the Virgin Mary, that the Son of the Father becomes Man.

One may wonder why the Son of the Father should become Man. This is stated above: for our sake and for our salvation. Now, the question arises: how would that be done? The answer is given by the next articles of our Creed: 'He was crucified... and suffered and was buried; he rose again on the third day...' His crucifixion is the death of our fallen nature. This dead nature of ours is buried and done away with once and for all, so that a new nature of Man is resurrected. Our baptism constitutes exactly that: the burial of the old self inside the water, which symbolises the grave of our old self and the resurrection of the new nature of Man, which is dressed in Christ and is therefore Christ-like. With the Holy Chrism we receive the gifts of the Holy Spirit and with the Holy Communion the union of Man and the Son of the Father is now a reality. Now everything is ready for the ascension into Heaven. This happens in the Person of the Son of the Father. And then, if we continue our course together with that of Jesus, we sit at the right hand of the Father in all of the Son's Glory. It is with this glory that the Son will come again. This second coming of His will not be to call the sinner to repentance and in all humility. His second coming will be in glory and in order to judge the living and the dead. His glory will not be the kind of glory that we are aware of. His glory will be the Light with which He is dressed in supreme simplicility. It is a kind of glory that we cannot imagine or comprehend.

His second coming will coincide with the complete destruction and fiery consumption of the universe. This world of time and space will come to its end. The end of this world will be the beginning of a new world which will be void of any change and wear and death. It will be the beginning of the Kingdom of God, which will have no end. This Kingdom has no relation whatsoever with the kingdoms of this world which are transient, frail, corrupt and evil.

Now, we come to the third Person of the Holy Trinity: the Holy Spirit. Naturally, no word is suitable for this Person as for any of the other two Persons. In English, they even call It the Holy Ghost. The third Person of the Holy Trinity is the Lord. That means that the Holy Spirit is God Himself, distinguished from the other two Persons. One cannot confuse it with the others. It is also the Giver of life. Without the Holy Spirit nothing would have any life in it.

As the Son is begotten from the Father, so the Holy Spirit proceeds from the Father. Western Christianity says that It proceeds from the Son as well. This is against the resolution of the third ecumenical synod which forbids any addition to, or deduction from the Creed. Filioque (= and from the Son) cannot stand theologically. This is explained above, when we were dealing with the Holy Spirit in detail. In a few words, the Holy Spirit is no less important, as the Filioque suggests. This is made absolutely clear from what the Creed says next. The Holy Spirit is worshipped and glorified together with the Father and the Son.

When we say that the prophets were the mouth of God, we actually refer to the third Person who spoke through them. The prophets are not commonplace writers. Of course, they write freely but with God's inspiration. This actually means that they speak with the inspiration that the Holy Spirit gives them. In fact, it is the Holy Spirit who speaks through the prophets. The prophets are the means by whom the Holy Spirit, and therefore God, speaks to us.

Before Jesus was crucified, resurrected and ascended into Heaven, He took care to establish His Church. The latter is the continuation of His work of dispensation. The Holy Spirit takes over His work and continues it through the ages. This Church is ***One, Holy, Catholic*** and ***Apostolic***.

It is *One* because the Church's founder is One. The Church is the Body of Christ and His Body cannot be broken into parts. The Church is *holy* because Her Founder is Holy and also Her members are holy because they are striving for perfection through their union with Christ with the Holy Communion.

The Church is also *catholic* because She embraces all people, all places and all time. Nobody, nowhere, nothing is excluded from the Church. To become a member is a matter of personal choice. The Church is also *apostolic* because it was founded by the apostles according to the commandment of Jesus to them.

With the Creed, we confess one baptism. Without baptism, we cannot become members of Christ's Body. This baptism cannot be more than one.

Something that we believe in is the expectation on our part of the resurrection of the dead. In other words, we do not believe that the grave is the end of Man's existence. We believe that resurrection follows our biological death. We believe that the resurrection will take place in time for those who are going to be found in this life. Of course, a change in the nature of Man will instantly take place. For the dead, who will actually belong to eternity and not to space and time, the resurrection takes place before the change that will come about to the living. St. Paul is very clear about that: 'and the dead in Christ will rise first' (I Thess. 4.16).

What will follow this event? This is given readily by the Creed: 'And the life of the age to come'. This life will be the one that will have no end and it will be in the Kingdom of God. This life here that we know will have an end and only the life that will remain will be the permanent and true life.

THE END